SAINTS + SINNERS
2021

NEW FICTION
FROM THE FESTIVAL

Visit us at www.boldstrokesbooks.com

SAINTS + SINNERS 2021

NEW FICTION
FROM THE FESTIVAL

edited by

Tracy Cunningham and Paul J. Willis

SAINTS + SINNERS

2021

SAINTS + SINNERS 2021
NEW FICTION FROM THE FESTIVAL
© 2021 By Saints & Sinners Literary Festival. All Rights Reserved.

ISBN 13: 978-1-63679-059-6

This Trade Paperback Original Is Published By
Bold Strokes Books, Inc.
P.O. Box 249
Valley Falls, NY 12185

First Edition: March 2021

Credits
Editors: Tracy Cunningham and Paul J. Willis
Production Design: Stacia Seaman
Cover Art by Timothy Cummings
Cover Design by Toan Nguyen

Acknowledgments

We'd like to thank:

The John Burton Harter Foundation for their continued support of the fiction contest and their generous support of the Saints and Sinners Literary Festival program.

Radclyffe, Sandy Lowe, and Bold Strokes Books for their talents in the production of our anthology and their sponsorship of the Saints and Sinners event.

Timothy Cummings, cover artist for the 2021 Saints and Sinners Literary Festival anthology and program book.

Amie M. Evans, whose editorial contributions over the years have informed and shaped the quality of these anthologies.

Everyone who has entered the contest and/or attended the Saints and Sinners Literary Festival over the last 18 years for their energy, ideas, and dedication in keeping the written LGBTQ word alive.

We'd also like to thank our 2020 participants, members, and sponsors for their understanding and support this past March when the pandemic forced the cancellation of our event two weeks before the start date.

Our Past Contest Winners

2020
Matthew Cherry "Big House"

2019
J. Marshall Freeman "The Grove of Mohini"

2018
Jeremy Schnotala "Sand Angels"

2017
J. Marshall Freeman "Curo the Filthmonger"

2016
Jerry Rabushka "Trumpet in D"

2015
Maureen Brady "Basketball Fever"

2014
Sally Bellerose "Corset"

2013
Sandra Gail Lambert "In a Chamber of My Heart"

2012
Jerry Rabushka "Wasted Courage"

2011
Sally Bellerose "Fishwives"

2010
Wayne Lee Gay "Ondine"

CONTENTS

INTRODUCTION

Salem West, 2021 Fiction Judge

Decades from now, people will look back on the year that was 2020. And when they do, the global pandemic will be the first thing—the most consuming thing—they see. But what also will register are the murky shadows of division: the dusky tinge of distrust and unfettered attacks on truth that salted the landscape. And, as their eyes gain focus, they will begin to pick out the individual contours of the things that shaped each of us. Masks. Social distancing. Black Lives Matter. QAnon. The deaths of Kobe Bryant, John Lewis, George Floyd. Phyllis Lyon, and Ruth Bader Ginsberg. The election of the first Black woman and Asian-American as Vice President of the United States. The world's oldest democracy teetering on the brink of collapse. The snail's pace delivery of COVID-19 vaccines. And Dolly Parton.

Those with vision and persistence will winnow in on images of the LGBT+ community. These will be brightly colored, yet confusing, at best. The rollback of transgender healthcare and discrimination rules. The extension of federal job protections for LGBT+ employees. The relaxation of blood donation restrictions for gay and bisexual men. New regulations allowing for expansion of faith-based discrimination. A third gender option on New Hampshire driver's licenses. The banning of conversion therapy in Virginia. Removal of the "gay panic" defense in Washington. And ratification of constitutional marriage equality in Nevada.

But what will they find when they begin to parse through our literature? They need look no further than this anthology and the wonderfully diverse and talented contributing authors who have shared snippets of their fears and revelations, their passions and compassions, their dark passengers and their best selves with us. I suspect they will hone in on the beguiling through line of self-discovery. It interweaves an inciting power of personal strength with awkward wants that are too compromising to be spoken, the overbearing weight of personal sacrifice, and the raging flood of broken promises.

The short stories collected here cover a wide spectrum of genres and time periods. They deliver memorable characters, even as they welcome you into their teeming worlds. They condense a vivid sense of a bigger story into smaller spaces before expanding to leave you full—remaining in your thoughts long after you have finished reading them.

I am confident that as you read these powerful stories, you will celebrate the creativity and verve of Colby Byrne, Laura Price Steele, Lisa Hines and all the extraordinary writers whose work fills the pages of this stunning collection—because when the year 2020 is thoughtfully considered through the refined arc of history, the world will surely know us by our words.

READY

Lisa Hines

Pedro stared at himself in the bathroom mirror in the hotel suite, floors above the ballroom where he was about to get married. He thought of the bodies rushing around below him, florists and caterers, hurrying to get it all just right. He thought about the people in all the floors stacked between him and his wedding, the building a giant concrete entremets, each layer containing multitudes. He wondered what they were doing at this exact moment. Were they laughing? Crying? Making love? Then, he flattened the lapels of his well-tailored suit, applied some cologne, and thought about his father.

As he made his way down the corridor he was struck by a sense of déjà vu. Not the exact moment, but the feeling. The stomach like a hive of bees, the cold damp of his hands, the fear that comes from something so personal being so public.

He was admittedly a bit distracted when he reached his mother's room. Otherwise he would have waited for a response when he knocked—a gentle tap—rather than just pushing the not-quite-latched door open and walking right in. Had he not been so lost in thought, he might have called out, or heard something that gave him pause, but instead he happened unannounced upon his mother and his bride-to-be.

There they were, the two women he loved most in the world, wrapped in lace and tulle, and smelling like all the flowers in a garden. They quickly broke apart, eyes wide and bodies stiff with surprise. Dust motes danced in the empty space between them, the only things moving in a room where just a moment ago, silhouetted by soft light filtering through the curtains, they had been delicately leaning into each other, kissing.

❖

Pedro's father loved music, clothes, and making his mother laugh. Whenever Pedro thought about him, Sam Cooke's "You Send Me," Chanel Bleu, and his mother's smile all came to him at once. Even as a memory, the man was a sensory experience.

Pedro always knew his mother and father's relationship was different. While his friends' parents seemed to have all this space between them—as they passed in the same room, or between the words spoken at the dinner table—his had proximity.

Even as a little boy, he recognized being outside of it. His parents loved him—and he felt their love—but he was one step removed from their closeness. If asked to describe his childhood *before*, it would be a loop of perching on the kitchen counter, his mother making tamales, and his father dancing around her. Twirling her. Dipping her. A smile and a laugh that spread all the way to her eyes.

And then one night, when he was eight years old, one dinner party changed everything.

The only time his parents seemed tense was when they were inviting outsiders in. Pedro didn't understand why they put themselves through it, and even asked once, but his father just gave him a wink and said, "How will all the ladies know how handsome you are if we don't have them over?" And Pedro laughed like it was a game because he wanted his father to believe it.

As his parents got ready, they grew quiet. His mother would put on clothing she never wore—long skirt and sleeves, high collar—and wipe the red from her mouth and the shadow from her eyes. Pedro sat on the bathroom counter, watching her dull herself, not understanding.

While his father got dressed in one of his many well-tailored suits, Pedro's mother dressed him. He knew she hated getting ready for these things, but he loved it, because he got to dress just like his father. He still remembered going with his father to the tailor. Standing still and getting poked with pins. Feeling the weight of fabric on his shoulders as the tailor and his father discussed the break of the pants and the hit of the cuff. The air smelling faintly of chalk. The whole thing, a ceremony.

Once he was dressed, and hair parted and glossy with pomade, his mother would usher him back into their bedroom. His father would turn around, smiling and nodding, "Ok, amigo! I see, I see!" And he'd do the high five that ended with a snap and then he'd turn to Pedro's mother and say, "Wait, something is missing, no?"

She would stand back and look at him like she was solving a puzzle, then snap her fingers. She would go to his father's vanity and hold out the midnight blue bottle. "A gentleman must smell nice too, no?" And then she would spray it into the air, and Pedro would walk into the cloud, feeling the soft kiss of vapor on his skin.

On this particular night, right as this moment passed, the first guest arrived. The doorbell was like a foreman entering the room. In an instant Pedro's father transformed from lithe and fluid to rigid and solid. His mother went from relaxed and confident, to erect and uncertain. Pedro looked from his mother's face, to his father's, their eyes saying, "We are brave."

The early moments of that dinner party felt like all the others. Husbands and wives arrived together, men all in suits, women dressed just like his mother. The men peeled off to join his father around the bar cart. The women headed to the kitchen. Pedro stood suspended in the middle, caught between his obligation to be a man, and his desire to be where all the warmth was. And then *he* appeared, a nightmare in Pedro's living room.

❖

Mr. Brennan was a serious man with a square jaw and severe haircut. Pedro had only seen him once before when he came to speak to their class. He talked a lot about the country, and how it had been dangerous and full of sin. He said a lot of those words that stung like lemon juice. Things that Pedro didn't understand, but that made him feel alone and sad.

When he got home from school that day he cried until his mother's blouse was wet with tears. When his body had finished heaving, his mother took his face in her hands and said, "Mi cielo, everyone feels sad and alone. Some people feel it inside, like you and me. Some people run from it. Running from it can look all kinds of ways. Sometimes it looks like eating too much. Sometimes it looks like spending too much. Sometimes it looks like hurting yourself. People like Mr. Brennan are the saddest kind. They're the ones who are so lonely and afraid they have to take things from other people to feel brave. We should always find love in our hearts for people like Mr. Brennan because they need it the most, and we have bravery to spare."

The men filtered into the dining room, and positioned themselves at alternating seats, Pedro's father at the head. He was the first to take a seat, then the other men followed in unison. Only then did the women emerge from the kitchen and take their seats to the left of their respective husbands.

The table was filled with platters of roasted meat, buttery potatoes, fresh-baked bread, all favorites of their guests. Although this food was much more decadent than their usual fare, Pedro found himself daydreaming about the smoky flavors, and savory sweet richness they usually ate. He knew that this, the way they were eating now, was better than the way they ate every day. He knew it had something to do with the people here being better than they were, but it was all very confusing. How do you reconcile something worse, being better, just because someone tells you so? From food to skin tone to countries, it seemed like everyone was always deciding what was good and what was bad.

While Pedro had been daydreaming, his father had led the table in prayer. The room filled with the sounds of silver scraping porcelain, and, "Please pass the potatoes," and the soft thud of platters returning to the tabletop. Pedro looked up to find Mr. Brennan sitting quiet as the sound reverberated around him.

Quiet like a forest before the report of a rifle.

Quiet like the stillness between heartbeats.

Pedro kept returning to his mother's words, and as the evening wound to a close, he went to search out Mr. Brennan. He wasn't sure why, or what he would do when he found him, but he thought maybe he could share some kindness, some courage.

Pedro wanted to help him.

Mr. Brennan wasn't in the living room with the few remaining guests. He wasn't in the kitchen, or in the bathroom. Pedro figured he must be collecting his and his wife's coats. As Pedro got closer to the coat room, he caught a whiff of his father's cologne, but maybe he was just smelling himself. Just outside the door he heard a whisper, his father's.

Then another voice, a man's, soft and tender like the purr of a cat.

Pedro didn't know this was a moment that meant more than any other, so he walked right into the coat room. First he saw his father's back, his navy suit and oil black hair. Then he was staring straight into the eyes that belonged to the second voice. A voice Pedro had only known to say cruel things.

A voice that lived inside a man who was too lonely to be brave.

A lonely man wrapped tenderly around his father.

Pedro watched those eyes transform from shock to terror to fury. He broke away from Pedro's father, who spun around to discover his son, standing still, not knowing what he'd done. As Mr. Brennan rushed from the room, Pedro's father tried to stop him.

"Robert, it's ok, he won't say anything."

But Mr. Brennan couldn't risk it, and the cornered-animal terror stopped Pedro's father from saying another word. It was Mr. Brennan who would say many more words, to many more people. Telling them all about Pedro's father just to shield himself.

Their lives got hard after that.

Pedro's friends stopped sitting with him at school. Kids he didn't even know would stare at him in the hallway and whisper as he walked by. Then one day in gym Pedro scored a goal and the goalie slammed his mitts to the ground and said something about Pedro's father. Even though Pedro knew he should show kindness and bravery to those who felt lonely and afraid, he momentarily forgot and broke the goalie's nose.

Pedro wasn't allowed back in school after that.

Meanwhile, his father became more and more of a shell. He never danced in the kitchen, or played music. His once tailored suits hung off his frame like he was a coat hanger. He never joked or laughed or gave Pedro the high five that ended with a snap. Pedro's mother tried to lift them all up, but there was no breaking through the fog. Until one evening his father came home from work and everything was different.

That night when he came in, his face was broken open with a smile. He squeezed Pedro tightly like he had been away on a long trip and had just returned. He put on some Sam Cooke and joined Pedro's mother in the kitchen. Pedro sat on the counter while they laughed and joked and danced the way they used to. They ate together, his father finishing two plates, and just outside the window it began to snow.

His father had to run out—he would be back before the weather got too bad—so Pedro sat on the back of the couch and watched out the front window as he pulled away. Pedro couldn't ever remember being so full of hope and love and all the good things in the world.

"Mama?"

"Si, mi cielo?"

"Can we bake a cake?"

Flour and sugar falling all around them.

Waiting.

And waiting.

And waiting.

Falling asleep at the table.

Being carried to bed in his mother's arms.

Still asleep the next morning when the policemen came to the door.

It was hard to spot his car under the layer of white, but they had found it. He had run a hose from the exhaust through the window. It would have been painless. Just slipped into a deep sleep with the snow falling all around him, like sugar.

It would be years before Pedro understood what happened.

He would remember the wake.

All the same men from the dinner party.

All in his house once again.

He would remember how hollow Mr. Brennan looked.

And then he wouldn't remember anything else for a long time.

If asked to describe his childhood *after*, there was nothing. Just a blank space where happiness once was.

His mother tried so hard to get him back. First, she thought routine would help, and the school agreed to take him since circumstances had changed. Even if he didn't remember the first day, his mother did. How she had to peel him out of bed. How she ignored the dampness of his pillowcase. How he didn't eat any breakfast and she was so scared as she dropped him off. How as his tiny hand gripped the door handle, she grabbed his shoulder and his little face, once so open but now so closed turned towards her.

"Remember. Bravery to spare."

She stared into his eyes, seeing something spark.

She mouthed, "Ready?"

He gave the smallest little nod, and eyes filling with tears, got out of the car.

Pedro did go back to school, and he did well and made friends, but the years that followed were filled with anger at all the wrong things, grief just bubbling over onto everything. His mother, trying to protect him, feared bringing him too close. Suddenly months had passed, years, without a tenderness between them. He had graduated high school, was practically a man. On the eve of his departure for college she stood at his bedroom door, marveling at this creature before her, this clone of her husband. She couldn't believe how distant they had become. She suddenly knew, standing at that threshold, that if he left without knowing the truth, she'd lose him forever.

They met when they were kids. He was sitting on his own at recess, making a dandelion crown while the kids around him screamed and ran and got grass stains on their trousers. She asked him to move so she could do cartwheels. Instead she got a halo of flowers and the best human she'd ever known. They were teenagers when they told each other they were gay. It was still ok then, but barely. They were allowed to be true to themselves for a time, but then everything changed. Knowing they could no longer be with anyone else, they decided to be together.

They spent years together dancing and laughing, and brought Pedro into the world. And even though life wasn't as full as it could have been, it was beautiful. Then Pedro's father and Mr. Brennan fell in love, and Mr. Brennan got scared.

"Pedro, your father loved us so much, and could have withstood it all, if it hadn't come from someone he loved."

Pedro left for college feeling clear for the first time in a long time. Fall break he came home to visit and noticed a change had come over his mother as well. She was starting to bloom again. And slowly over the course of that year, from the tail end of summer through fall and winter and back into spring, she re-emerged as herself. When he came home the following summer to see her, she greeted him in her black cowboy boots and vintage denim, a starched white button-down showing her browned sternum tanned like leather under all her favorite turquoise. Her hair had gone silver, but her perfectly red lips welcomed him inside and introduced him to the woman she loved.

"Jesus Cristo, mama! Cierre la puerta! Anyone could have seen you!"

"I'm sorry, I'm sorry, mi cielo! You're right."

"It's time to head down."

Pedro watched his mother lovingly tuck a lock of hair behind the bride's ear, extended his arm, and escorted her down to their wedding.

Once he met Jane, and saw the reason for his mother's blooming, the arrangement was a no-brainer. He would never have participated in marriage anyway. Not in this world. Not their way. It was his idea, Jane being not too far from his own age. He began courting her publicly, moving back home after graduation to care for his poor widowed mother. And Jane, what a saint, what a woman, to be willing to live with her mother-in-law after the wedding.

His mother was hesitant at first. "Pedro, mi cielo, what about your love? What about your life?" He reminded her of the time when she told him the whole truth. How, when asked how she and his father could have endured she shrugged and said, "Sometimes you have to be strict with yourself to be generous with others."

The guests had long been seated.

His mother left him at the end of the aisle.

The room vibrated with love and hope and all the best things in the world.

The music started.

The bride appeared to the transcendent voice of Sam Cooke.

Pedro and his mother locked eyes, and as hers filled with tears, he mouthed, "Ready?"

This story was inspired by the Reedsy.com prompt, "Twenty minutes before you are about to get married, you find your mother and your fiancé kissing passionately."

HOSPITALITY

TJ Barnes

Tye may be too much for some people to take, but it's not an act. It's her nature to wake up happy. She sets her alarm to go off early every day so she can lie in bed and think about everything she's going to do with her life, all the plans she constantly changes because there are so many possibilities spinning in her brain that it's hard to know what to take on first. She craves vision. It needs time to form. In the meantime, she gets ready for work by cheerfully choosing clothes, showering, applying makeup, and once she's put together, making strong coffee. She hardly ever eats breakfast. Today she allows herself exactly five strawberries. She's afraid of gaining weight, and since she can't skip lunch because she's too hungry by that point in her shift, she makes it through the first half of her day on caffeine. She loves being on the front desk at the Best Western. She loves interacting with people, and she's good at it. People are everything.

The lobby is empty when she arrives, as usual. It's still dark out, with only the glowing lamps beside each room's door visible across the cracked asphalt parking lot, shimmering with yesterday's rain. She will put on the complimentary coffee for check-in, go over the list of which rooms are vacating so she can make sure everything is well coordinated with housekeeping, and turn on the welcome video that plays on an endless loop. She pauses in front of the monitor though she's seen this ad about a million times, smiling to think *yeah,* this is where she lives, if anyone would believe it. She knows she'll leave one day, but she doesn't spend much time on that, only her allowed daydreaming in bed. Her mom is getting old too fast, the way time speeds up for some people more than others, suddenly accelerating before stopping altogether. She is Tye's other job. Any good daughter's job. Besides, is she really in a hurry to leave a place where people are so friendly?

After a montage of other Best Westerns in far more exotic places, a rainbow banner scrolls across the screen. *Don't forget to check out Heinz Heaven! Home of the World's Largest BLT! Presidents have eaten here!* It costs good money for perpetual placement in the lobby, though she has no idea how much. Management makes those decisions. At least it's something for guests to look at while they wait to check in or out, and Heinz Heaven might be the only claim to fame that Franklich, Michigan will ever have. Otherwise, they're nothing but a random stop between Flint and the Mackinac Bridge for weary tourists headed to the UP. She could never eat one of those monstrous sandwiches by herself, but for other people, why not? Whatever floats their boats. Eat without judgment. Live without judgment. Tye tries her best. Most of the people in the video are huge, but it's what she would tactfully call *Midwestern plump.* She knows there is a radically different scale in places like New York City, where five pounds extra is a step away from obesity. She brushes her hand across her abdomen and down over one hip, smoothing her skirt. Safe for another day, still resting at her high school weight. Meanwhile, the onscreen diners are presented overflowing, steaming platters. The camera zooms in on their faces. Eyes widen. They shake their heads in disbelief. *Hey, who ordered this thing anyway? A full pound of bacon in every sandwich! That's crazy!* At the end, there's a catchy jingle—it hasn't changed in years—and the restaurant's rainbow logo reappears over a sequence of flushed customers, patting swollen bellies and pointing to empty plates. It's sort of disgusting, but Tye can't help having a soft spot for the place where she grew up.

Her first guest of the day looks like he might be a truck driver. Tye makes a sport of guessing people's occupations or filling in the imaginary details of their lives. It's one of the most fun things about her job. Sometimes she surprises them. "Good morning, sir," she says. "Checking in?"

"Yeah." The man stares down at the countertop.

Tye thinks she hears a snort. He doesn't seem like he wants to be surprised by anything. "And the name is?"

"I don't have a reservation," the guy says, digging a yellowed finger into one ear. "You got a room for today? I'll be leaving come night. Got a long drive. I didn't see no truck parking specified. I put my rig over on the far side of the lot. I ain't blocking nobody."

She nailed it. Her gifts of perception are sure to give her an edge no matter where she ends up in life. "That's totally fine," she says. "Of course we have a room for you. We'll have to charge you for a full night. Is that all right? Best Western has no such thing as a day rate."

"No hookers," the driver says, laughing.

Tye smiles. "Oh, I don't make the rules." She is sure she hears him snort.

"Yeah," he says under his breath. "You people."

She imagines he must be horribly tired, not rude, and hands over a paper for him to sign, then runs his credit card and returns it to him.

"Room 128, just outside," she says. "Around the corner to your left and all the way down to the end. You'll have a lot of quiet there. I hope you enjoy your stay!"

He swipes the card key off the counter and turns away without answering.

By now the sun has begun its steady climb to life. The picture window opposite her is blazing orange, allowing a growing shard of startling white to cut across the carpet. She loves this time of day, when the brightness from outside makes her lobby sparkle. She could be anywhere in the world in this light. Los Angeles, New York, Paris. Or closer. Chicago. Ann Arbor. Madison. Any of those places might be possible one day, once her mother no longer needs her. Just because she hadn't gone to college doesn't mean she might not enjoy living in a place where she could rub up against fresh ideas and smart people who share her general creativity and curiosity. New friends with old souls, something like that. Until then, Tye's mission is to think big inside the smallish confines of her present nest, where people who are traveling for all sorts of reasons, happy and sad, depend on her to make the journey easier.

Two young men and a little girl are next to approach, all holding hands. Tye suspects they're from a big city. The men are wearing skinny jeans that don't bag around the ankles and expensive looking leather shoes with no socks. She can tell what they want from their shared expression, and it pleases her for them not to have to ask. "The breakfast buffet is just through there," she says, pointing past the video monitor to a long bar with a partition on one side to separate it from the hallway to the pool. Tye is proud of what awaits this party of three and everyone else who will follow them out of bed and into the day, continuing their respective road trips. She can almost see the neat rows of offerings from where she stands: Cereal (multiple kinds), toast (multiple kinds), yogurt (multiple kinds), fruit (bananas and apples), a divided stainless steel vat with scrambled eggs on one side, bacon and sausage patties on the other, and a make-your-own waffle station.

"Help yourself to everything, and enjoy your morning!" Tye says. "One of the girls is always back there if you need anything. Just ask, okay?"

"She has a bad voice," the little girl says, looking up at one of the men. "What's wrong with it?"

"Sweetheart," the other man says, "everyone has a different voice."

He looks at Tye, and she smiles instantly, no offense taken. Who would have thought, two dads, stopping in Franklich. She can't help wondering where they are going from here, and whether it will be as friendly. She hopes so. They must have learned by now to go where they're wanted and avoid the other places. Beautiful child, sweet parents. It's a shame they can't feel at home everywhere in the world.

Tye isn't bothered by much. She learned long ago to brush off the things that hurt her and concentrate instead on what makes her feel good. This job, the people she meets, the morning light, what she might do when she has more money, and even her mother, this chance to grow closer to her, which has been hard and would have never happened had she not gotten bad sick. Tye feels lucky. She could be much worse off than she is. She knows that two thirds of the world's population live in cities, but she lives here, in Franklich, Michigan, where people know her. They also know her mother, and before he left, her father, too. Knowledge is power, she's always heard. Part of her power comes from being known.

She passes the rest of her morning by answering the phone. *Yes, we have plenty of available rooms. Yes, we offer discounts for AAA and AARP. Yes, I'm happy to say we are a pet friendly hotel, for a small charge. Yes, we have a pool—it's indoor and heated. Our winters are cold! No, we don't have a restaurant, but we do serve a complimentary breakfast, and it's really good. No, I won't be on the desk this evening, but I'll make sure that whoever is here knows that you are arriving late,*

I promise. Her calls end with a perky *No problem!* It's really not an effort, she would say if asked. Whenever thanked, *No problem!*

She chooses the drive-through at Wendy's for lunch. She tries to alternate among her regular places to keep from getting bored. Today she'll get extra fries for her mom. She can pop them in the microwave later and serve them with the leftover gumbo she made last week when she'd been inspired by finding frozen shrimp on sale. As she pulls up to the pickup window, she's happy just thinking about other favorite recipes she simply must find time to prepare. She makes a mental note to check out some cookbooks from the library. She'll start experimenting with new dishes to get her mother to eat more. Lately, it hasn't been easy.

"Asian Cashew Chicken Salad—half size, two small fries, and ice water?" a teenage boy says through the sliding glass.

"That's me," Tye says. She hands him a ten-dollar bill.

When he gives back her few cents change, she peeks inside the bag. "Would you mind giving me some more ketchup? I love it."

He shuts the window and walks away.

She is glad not to be a teenager now. At least she didn't have social media to deal with when she was growing up. The pressure of seeing yourself all the time. And being seen. Her generation thought flip phones were a big deal. She's watched enough psychologists on *Good Morning, America* to know how stressed out kids are.

The boy opens the window and drops two packets of ketchup into her outstretched hand, then slams the glass shut again without speaking.

He's sad, she thinks. She sees him point her out to another order taker as she puts the car into gear. She feels sorry for him. He's probably like every teenage boy, wanting sex and not getting it, or sitting on top of anger that he can't talk about, mainly because he wants to be a man. Poor kid. She shouldn't expect him to be polite. There's probably no one in his life who is polite to him.

She eats her lunch on a picnic table in the small grass plot outside the motel lobby's floor-to-ceiling window. She can see her colleague Lucretia talking to a rotund older woman who is gesturing wildly with her hands. Lucretia can handle her, Tye is certain. They have different styles—God knows, the understatement of the century—but Tye likes her. They're not girlfriends outside of work, but when they're both on the same shift, they definitely catch a few laughs together. Tye likes to think it's another of her gifts, making people feel comfortable enough to laugh.

"Girl, you are not gonna believe this one," Lucretia says, as soon as Tye comes inside.

"Wait, not yet," Tye answers. "Let me put this in the fridge." She folds over the white paper sack to make it as compact as possible without crushing her mom's fries. As soon as she comes back around to the front desk, Lucretia starts in on one of her stories.

"So, that woman comes in here all on fire, talking about she found a condom on the grass and shouldn't have to pay for her room. And I say, ma'am was it in your way, was it outside your room, and she says, no she saw it when she was walking her dog Tippy or Dippy or something."

"Well, it *is* gross, Lucretia. She looked old."

"You're as bad as her. Grow up, I wanted to say. It wasn't in your room. It wasn't in your bed. You don't even know if one of the guests is the one put it there, walking that ratty dog way over on the edge of the property. Could have been anybody doing the nasty."

"I probably would have given her a courtesy discount or something, just to keep her happy."

"Well, let me tell you I did not offer her no damn thing the way she was talking to me. But thank you Jesus, I was not rude. I'm just blowing off steam with you, you know what I'm saying?"

"I do, honey. It's over. She's gone. We'll never see her again. If we do, it's an opportunity, I guess. That's how I look at it."

"I'm thinking she's the type gonna write a complaint, and Tye, you know I need this job."

"Don't worry about something that hasn't happened yet. I've got your back. I saw the whole thing even if I didn't hear it."

Lucretia clucks her tongue. "That's what I will never understand about you, Tye, how you're so calm all the time. It looks to me like you ought to get fired up about all kind of stuff."

"Oh honey, I can if I need to," Tye says, grinning, showing big white teeth on top. "Well, that mess just about wore me out. I've got two more hours, and then I'm gonna have to go home and take me a nap."

"You should, you deserve it. I won't say a word if you want to slip out early."

"Why're you being so nice? Did you get yourself a little something fine last night you don't want to tell me about?"

"Now you know if I did, I couldn't wait to tell you."

"I hope. All I know is you're looking good, Tye, and you need somebody to make you feel good, too. You got to get out there."

"Thank you, baby. I'm trying."

"Good. Now let me get back in that office and do my paperwork. Lord knows I want to get my ass out of here on time."

Tye likes the way Lucretia compliments her on her wardrobe, her hair. She's always got something nice to say about how Tye looks. She makes an effort, Tye thinks, and it inspires her. How hard is it to make an effort? Isn't it something everyone could learn to do? Just letting someone know that she looks good? It could change the whole world.

When she gets home around four o'clock, her mother is watching reruns of *Family Feud*. She looks up as if surprised to see her, even though this is the same time Tye comes in almost every afternoon. "How was your day, sweetheart?" she asks, turning down the volume on the remote.

Tye drops her purse on the kitchen counter and takes off her heels. "Oh, fine. Tiring, you know, in a good way though. How about you?"

"You know, I think I felt better today. I got up and walked for a few minutes. Then I got winded, but at least I did it."

"That's wonderful, Mama! See there, what did the doctor tell you about walking? It's good for your heart."

"Not that it changes anything else."

"Now stop that," Tye says, sitting down on the sofa beside her mother. "We caught this early. It's very treatable. Let's keep our attitude up. Exercise always helps with attitude. I think I'm going to run to the mall after dinner. Is there anything special you want? How about some of that nice honeysuckle liquid soap they've got at the bath outlet?"

"I've got plenty of that still left. But you can surprise me with something. If you want to. But you don't have to."

Tye kisses her mother on top of the head. She smells a mixture of oil and perspiration. She needs a shampoo. That will be tomorrow's chore as soon as she gets home. She pads down the short hall into her bedroom and opens the closet. She doesn't really need any new clothes, but she would like to find something a little special that she could wear when she goes out, which she is planning to do more of soon. She hasn't felt very confident going to bars, but she doesn't know where else to go at her age. She's not even thirty yet, but it's not as if any people she knows are giving parties, at least not the kind of party where someone goes to meet other people, the dating kind of people. She knows her options are limited, but she is hopeful that someone she knows might know someone else, that kind of thing, and you never know when that might happen. Until it does, there's no way she can entertain anyone here with her mom around.

Tye goes to the mirror over her dresser and takes down her ponytail, brushing her black hair in long, slow strokes. She is guilty of wanting her mother to get well enough so she can move out and have her own place, but she doesn't want to leave her the way her father did. Tye made a promise to herself that she would not think about this subject outside of these four walls. Her bedroom was her safe house, as if no one was allowed to know where it was, no one was allowed to enter or exit without clearance. She pulls out a low cut lavender top with a short matching skirt. Her father had slapped her across the face the first time he saw her in this. A month later, jobless, he was gone. She saved the outfit to spite his memory.

Going to the mall all alone is still a bit of an experiment, but she's getting bolder. She can lose herself there in the color and noise. She can blend right in, walking alongside other people with bags, or sitting down on a bench with an ice cream cone to take it all in. She is part of this huge current, and as much as she loves the cocoon of the Best Western, she also enjoys doing what other women do, shopping for things on sale, buying little gifts for special occasions that don't yet exist, hoarding them for when the right moment presents itself, and finding something perfect to wear that is so very irresistible that she doesn't try to resist.

"Thank you for making this," her mother says, after taking three bites of gumbo and pushing the bowl away.

"Oh Mama, you need to eat more. Look what I brought." She whisks a Pyrex bowl of French fries from the microwave and squirts great swirls of ketchup all over them. "You'll have some of these, I know, won't you?"

She pours herself another glass of Diet Coke and happily watches her mother eat, reaching across the table from time to time to dab red from the corners of her mouth. When her mother swipes her hand away, Tye says, "Oh, you quit that right now. You look like a vampire."

She will leave the dishes undone until she gets back. She undresses her mother and helps her into pajamas. Evening is not the best time for baths. They are both usually too tired. She will bathe her again on her day off.

"You go on to sleep," Tye says. "I'm going to lock up everything. I'll be back in an hour or two. You know me, I have to get my sleep if I'm going to be worth anything tomorrow!"

Her mother beckons her from the bed, and when she leans close, kisses her on the cheek. "Enjoy yourself. Don't worry about me. I want you to enjoy your life," she says.

"I know, Mama," Tye whispers. "I do."

She scores a fantastic parking space outside Dillard's, her favorite store. It's going to be a perfect night, she can tell. She has been saving up her money for Clinique. It really is the best brand because it's effective but doesn't have an off-putting fragrance that would interfere with her perfume. She approaches a pristine glass counter where a pretty young blond woman with candy apple lips is dressed in a white lab coat. The woman busies herself with papers on a clipboard. Tye waits patiently for her to finish whatever she is doing, but she doesn't seem to notice.

"Excuse me," Tye says. "Could you help me?"

"What are you looking for?" the woman says, pushing her glasses higher on her nose.

"I think I'd like to try a few different things if you don't mind," Tye says, seating herself on one of the white pleather padded stools.

"We don't really do a lot of sampling or makeover stuff at night," the saleswoman says. "Maybe you could come during the day? I'm here by myself right now, so I need to be available to other customers."

"Oh, I didn't know," Tye says. "Maybe you have some trial sizes I could take home?"

"I'll check. Did you want to purchase something?"

"I think so, yes. Some liquid base," Tye says. "I don't want to go too dark, but…"

"I think this is what I would recommend for your type," the woman says, placing a green box on the counter. It costs more than a week of Tye's lunches. "We don't have a lot of specialty shades in stock," the clerk continues. "Do you think this will work for you?"

Tye wants it to work. It's Clinique, and that's what she wants, and they're supposed to have a product for every woman, so she hands over her debit card. The woman brings back her receipt and asks whether she wants a bag or just to put it in her purse. Tye does want a bag, a shiny little green bag with satiny white rope handles that she can carry while she continues her shopping. The woman puts the bag on the counter and plops the box of base inside.

"Any samples?" Tye asks.

"Oh, I'm so sorry, I checked and we're out."

"Don't worry, that's okay!" Tye says. "Thank you so much. I know this will work out for me." She taps the little shopping bag and walks away, feeling happy with what she's done, what she has.

She strolls past Cinnabon, Doolittle's Party Supply, The Gap, Sunglass Hut, and Zales Jewelers, swinging her tiny bag, pausing to consider what else she might buy if she could. She doesn't need anything, but it's still fun. She waves to two small children eating popcorn, she smiles at an elderly lady in a wheelchair, she stops at BodyWorks and buys a small tube of lilac hand cream for her mother. She loves these simple pleasures. It's not hard for her to have a good time. Her father should see her now. People would be so much happier if they didn't pay attention to all that's bad in the world. She chooses not to focus on the negative, and it has made all the difference.

Which is why she doesn't realize what hits her when she's in the ladies room. She doesn't suspect that someone has flung open a stall door to knock her against the wall. She doesn't see the two men in baseball caps, with no reason to be there. She doesn't see what they see, the shoulders that once belonged to a sixteen-year-old quarterback, the thick biceps that she has hidden with a loose cotton sweater until they rip it off, the dark shadow that graces her chin and jawline, demanding to be noticed under the smear of fleshy cover-up, the Adam's apple that is a target for one of their punches, the dirt under the nails on her large hands, with veins running along their backs, the big face and big feet, swelling inside low black pumps in size eleven. She doesn't see what they see because she is happy. Blind in the falling darkness, she doesn't see their faces, contorted with laughter. They must be happy, too. Hospitality matters. She made them happy by being herself. She doesn't see them leave, stomping on her purchases, but she recognizes the smell of lilacs. Her mother will be so surprised. Small gifts always make her cry. Lying on the cold tile floor, with blood pooling around her head, she clutches the Clinique bag to her chest. For a few seconds, comfort. And in the sudden bright light that follows the blackness, too bright to be another Best Western sunrise, she doesn't yet see that she will never be alone again.

THE LOST OBJECT EXERCISE

Bill Gaythwaite

Joe and I were on the roof deck of the beach house trying to make out some skywriting in the distance. It was an ad for a casino, but some of the letters appeared to be inverted. We made a few jokes about dyslexic pilots and then Joe volunteered some things he knew about the skywriting process—how the smoke is made from very watery oil injected into a heater and how sometimes the plane has to fly upside down. I wondered if any of this, the jokes or Joe's facts, would be decent subjects for dinner. We were told it would be family style tonight, with everyone pitching in to make the meal and then we would all have to sit down and eat together. I didn't want there to be any long silences.

We'd been invited to Fire Island for the weekend and had arrived that morning, feeling geriatric and irrelevant on a ferry boat filled with half-dressed, beautiful young men. Henry List, the art historian, and Joe's second cousin, had been renting a house in the Pines for many summers, a stunning three story structure with walls of glass facing the ocean and a pool the size of a small pond. It was a last minute invitation for us. I assumed somebody else had backed out. Joe and Henry got on well enough (everybody loved my husband) but we'd never been invited out to the island before and we rarely saw Henry under any circumstances. Joe and I were the only couple. The other guests were single, older men, friends of Henry's. He knew them from AA. Henry was a recovering alcoholic with over twenty years sober. They were all on the other end of the island now, attending a 12-step meeting, while Joe and I were lounging on the roof.

We'd been introduced to the others that morning, when we arrived at the house. Alan was a freelance food stylist who lived near Fort Tryon Park and Gerald was a masseur with a celebrity clientele. The third man was named Martin Macduff and I had hustled and robbed him thirty-two years before, when I was twenty-three years old.

Thankfully, there was no click of recognition when Martin shook my hand. I had gained thirty pounds since then and grown a thick beard, which was now mostly grey. I didn't turn heads on the street anymore (those days were long gone) but occasionally someone from the hotel where I worked planning events would refer to me as distinguished-looking, a compliment I particularly despised, given my glossy, attention-pulling youth.

So Martin hadn't placed me, but I knew him immediately. Henry, during the hasty introductions, had told us that he managed a famous bookstore in the Village. This is what Martin had been doing back when I first met him. Plus, I remembered his name. Martin Macduff. Macduff was the character who killed Macbeth, the pivotal antagonist in the play, the moral center to the whole thing. Martin had told me all that the night we met. Since I didn't have much of an education (I'd barely graduated from a shitty college in Ohio) and because I had zero interest in Shakespeare, it was pointless to pretend familiarity with the information. It was easier to hang on Martin's every word and fix him with an appreciative gaze as he improved my knowledge. This, I figured, was the best chance to keep him interested that night, though my looks had probably already sealed the deal.

Martin might have thought I was more literate than I was because we'd met in a bookstore, though I'd really only stepped in to get out of the cold. I remember it was a few days before Christmas and the store bustled with a combination of good cheer and gift-giving panic. Chloe, my roommate, a crazy, egotistical actress I'd known from that shitty college, had booked a long-term gig doing theatrical murder mysteries on cruise ships. She had sublet our apartment out from underneath me that afternoon. We'd had a scorching scene about it and now my bags were stashed in a storage locker at Port Authority. I had no other place to stay that night and had about $60 in my pocket. I didn't have a job anymore either. I'd been fired the previous week. The answering service where I worked had let me go because they didn't like my phone manner, which had been described as *terse*. I'd asked for a second chance, but not very pleasantly, and so they'd still given me the boot.

I was weighing my options, such as they were, when Martin approached me. I was standing in front of a large display of books featuring the works of Edith Wharton. The expression on my face must have looked searching and confused, because Martin sidled up next to me and began giving me a brief rundown of the author's career, her high society lineage and Paris salon. I noticed he was pipe-cleaner skinny and balding, adrift somewhere in his thirties. Normally I wouldn't have acknowledged him at all. I'd only been in the city a few months, but long enough to be aware of my enviable place in the gay pecking order—given my youth and surfer boy looks. In other words, I was a little jerk. Actually, I didn't know as much as I thought I did. When I'd arrived in New York to live with Chloe (a roommate had bailed on her and she'd summoned me from my home in Pennsylvania) she'd told me that a guy like me might do well for himself in the city if I played my cards right. I didn't exactly know what she was telling me, other than that good looks tended to open doors. That part I already knew. There were examples of this everywhere. Just recently one of the other operators at the service, a genial, beefcake type had met some promising director at a casting call and now they were living together. This guy had walked into a room, read for a part and then his life had changed. I'm not sure if the same sense of opportunity was dancing around in my head when skinny Martin came up to me in the bookstore, but I was aware of a kind of internal adjustment. I looked into Martin's eyes and smiled broadly as he spoke. I had large, bright teeth, in the style of the Osmonds or the Kennedys. People either liked my grin or else they were reminded of Mormon fanaticism and family tragedy. I could see that Martin fell into the former category. I noticed the spark of genuine interest in his face as he spewed out more random details about *The Age of Innocence* and *Ethan Frome*. It wasn't so difficult, feigning concentration and grinning like a lunatic, to finagle a dinner invitation out of him. His shift was ending soon and he wondered if I might like to continue our conversation across the street at *The Leaning Tower of Pizza*.

"That would be smashing," I said pretentiously, as if I was some smiling British tourist.

As I waited around for Martin to finish up, I thought I might even ladle in a slight accent over dinner. Chloe would sometimes adopt an accent and pretend she was someone else for an entire day, as she made her way around the city or waited on customers at a 50s themed diner where she used to work, taking orders in a poodle-skirt.

"I like to take a break from myself every once in a while," she would tell me, explaining these invented personas, "and it's good training too."

Chloe had done a year at the Neighborhood Playhouse (it was rolling admission) but she hadn't made the cut and been asked back for serious study after that. I'd seen her do some accents on the stage too (a few showcases in church basements) but her dialect work was usually all over the map, a mulligan stew of hard consonants and flat vowels. I decided against changing my vocal patterns that night, because I probably couldn't have done any better than that.

I remember we left the bookstore and walked across the street to the small, lively restaurant, where the staff all seemed to know Martin. They greeted him with practiced delight, as we were led to a table in the back. I wondered, cynically, how many other confused-looking young customers he'd brought over here after his shifts. I even made a joke about that, which Martin didn't seem to appreciate. He blushed and blinked rapidly. I'd either struck a nerve or maybe my predatory suspicions had been all wrong.

"They know me here," Martin then said, unnecessarily, as the waiter came over with a bottle of wine, before we'd even opened our menus.

"I don't drink," I told him, apologetically, when he tried to pour me a glass.

"Not at all?" Martin asked, looking surprised and slightly crestfallen.

"Nope," I said. "I've never really liked the taste or how it makes me feel."

It was easier to say this than get into a discussion of my home life, where my father's drunkenness had the impact and consequences of a blowtorch. I'd witnessed enough lurching calamity growing up (my dad's lost jobs, his blackouts, my mother's zombie-like stoicism) not to gamble with my own predispositions. I refused to touch the stuff. In college, I was the only guy drinking soda at keg parties. But I certainly wasn't going to share all that with a stranger trying to get in my pants. In fact, I hadn't even given Martin my real name.

"I'm Caleb," I'd told him, before we'd left the bookstore.

"Lovely to meet you, Caleb. I'm Martin Macduff."

Caleb was a name I'd always liked, so biblical and forthright. I guess introducing myself like that suggests I already had some strategy for deception laid out for the evening, but it's difficult to remember my precise thoughts and motivations. At the restaurant, Martin poured some wine for himself and gave the waiter our orders. Then he told me about his favorite authors. I remember he especially admired Sinclair Lewis, thinking he was underrated. That might have been true, as I hadn't even heard of him. The waiter came back to fuss over us and then backed away geisha-style, as if Martin was some visiting dignitary and not just a glorified clerk from across the street. This must have been when Martin brought up the business about Macduff. I don't recall the exact chronology of our conversation over dinner. At some point, though, he got around to asking a few questions about me. He watched me with such hungry anticipation. Maybe that's what put some of the fabrication in motion. He was giving me such indulgent, hopeful smiles. I told him I was from California, a place I'd never even been. I told him my family was sort of in the movie business. My father worked for MGM as an accountant, I said, and my mother had been a contract player at the studio before she retired to have me. I described a sunny, frolicking childhood near the ocean. I'd made all this up. I figured it might charm him if I appeared accidentally glamorous.

In reality, at that moment, my father was probably passed out on the sofa in the house my parents rented outside Harrisburg; with my long-suffering mother shuffling gloomily through the rooms after attending evening Mass. It was a familiar scene I remembered from growing up and beyond. I had moved back home for a while after college. I'd been working in a hardware store in the neighborhood with no real plans for my future. I'd been an indifferent, listless student and I had no well of ambition to draw from either. I didn't know what I was going to do. Until Chloe had tracked me down and told me she needed a roommate in New York. When Martin asked me specifically what had brought me to the city, I couldn't explain that mixture of escape and reinvention, so I told him I planned to be an actor, stealing details from Chloe's personal narrative, including her acting school and prickly determination.

"Following in your mom's footsteps," Martin said, and it took me a second to realize he was referring to my fake mother's Hollywood past.

"Yes," I stammered, "but I see myself more on the stage."

"Well, you're good-looking enough for film and television. That's for sure," Martin said, as he poured himself more wine. He was blushing again too.

"Oh, thanks," I responded, lowering my eyes in modesty.

I did keep one thing from my real life. I told him about my work at the answering service, though I didn't mention I'd been fired. There was a tiny bit of allure attached to this job, because there were some celebrities on the service and others who called in to leave messages. I'd spoken to Faye Dunaway once and Al Pacino. I told Martin this and he seemed almost impressed.

The waiter brought a second bottle of wine and Martin ordered us banana pudding for dessert, which arrived in thimble-sized cups. Then Martin asked about my acting classes, and so I mentioned *The Lost Object Exercise*, something Chloe had recently explained to me. You had to pretend you'd misplaced the most precious object you ever owned, and then go about conveying the emotion you were feeling, without uttering a single sound. When Martin nodded his thoughtful approval at this, I went on. I made up a story about performing a scene from *Equus* for my audition technique class while stark naked. Chloe told me this had actually happened. One of her classmates, a hunky flirt, had flexed and posed his way through a long monologue, as everyone either gaped or looked away. I knew this was a teasing and manipulative detail to wave in front of Martin. His eyes widened and his whole head flushed pink. He was quite drunk by then. After the meal was finished, Martin paid the check, leaving an enormous tip, which explained his popularity with the staff. Then he suggested we go back to his place.

"Do me the honor," he said, rather desperately I thought.

This was obviously what I'd been after, but still I deliberated. I hadn't been in the city long enough to make any real friends, so there was no one I could crash with even for a night or two, and those new tenants, the ones subletting, had already moved into Chloe's apartment. I refused to call home or head back to Pennsylvania. My father had been furious that I'd moved out because he'd been counting on my rent payment. He'd probably already found a boarder, some lost soul, as he'd done while I was away at college. What other options did I have on this particular night?

"Sure," I told Martin. "Let's go."

❖

Joe stood up from his Adirondack chair and walked to the edge of the roof deck, where he let out a low whistle. I got up and joined him. There were a dozen or so hot, young guys from the house next door, lolling by the pool in their Speedos. We had a bird's eye view.

"Welcome to the candy store," Joe said, trying to amuse me, one of his familiar habits.

His leering comment was harmless enough, given that we were now a long married suburban couple in our fifties with a grown daughter. Ellie was in Italy, doing graduate work in art restoration at the Uffizi. (Joe's sister had been our surrogate.) And Henry, in fact, had been helpful with our daughter's grad school applications.

We watched the boys in the other house—wistfully, I suppose. Joe was never the philandering type, but I'd had a risky affair once, with one of the "straight" dads at Ellie's elementary school. Our kids were in different grades and didn't really know each other, so it wasn't as sordid as it might have been, but it was sordid enough. This man pursued me so urgently and with such abandon it took my breath away. It would crush Joe to know anything about this, even though it has been over and done with for fifteen years. I'd never told Joe about what happened with Martin either. It would have made a difference to him. Joe tended to believe people were moral and upright until he'd been presented with incontrovertible evidence to the contrary. He'd been giving me the benefit of the doubt ever since we met. I used to wonder if his moral certitude (along with my suburban boredom and male vanity) was one of the things that pushed me into that long ago affair, but that's probably too complicated to really decipher at this late date, and not fair to Joe who has always loved me in his knee-jerk way.

❖

As we left the restaurant, Martin and I braced ourselves against a swirling, icy wind. It had turned bitter cold since we'd been inside. This might have sobered Martin up some. His voice was less slurry anyway, as we began to walk toward his apartment, as he began to tell me about his mother who was very ill. She had lymphoma, he said, and didn't have long to live. His father had died in a boating accident long before, when he was a teenager.

"I'll be an orphan," he laughed in a weary, hollow way, "a middle-aged orphan."

His mom had given Martin and his sister (who lived near her in Seattle) some cash for Christmas. Might as well have some of it now, she'd said in a note, and not wait for the will. She'd packed Martin's money up in a gift box and sent it to him special delivery. It had arrived that day, Martin said, though you weren't supposed to send cash through the mail, so she'd taken a real chance.

"The chemo must have fried her brain," he whispered grimly.

Martin lived on the 4th floor of a graffiti covered building near the Bowery. An odor of cat piss hit me when we walked through the door of his apartment, my eyes welling up momentarily from the smell, though I never saw a cat. It was a dark and cluttered studio with an unmade futon in the corner, books and papers strewn on all the surfaces and empty liquor bottles scattered around the kitchen, which was really just a row of appliances lined up against the wall. The mess reminded me of the chaos at home in Pennsylvania. I preferred things streamlined and orderly in my own life. Chloe and I actually got along in this regard. Our apartment in Williamsburg wasn't anything palatial, but at least it was clean and neat, which is probably the reason she'd been able to sublet it so fast.

"Sorry about the place," Martin said, making a sweeping gesture towards everything. "Wasn't exactly expecting company."

He sounded slurry again. He went immediately to the freezer and pulled out a bottle of vodka.

"Want a drink?"

"I don't drink," I said, but not as sweetly as I'd said it in the restaurant.

"Oh, that's right. But do you mind if I do?" he asked, as he was pouring himself a large glass.

I noticed Martin's hand was shaking. I wondered if he was nervous about my being there or if this was just a byproduct related to the heavy drinking. After growing up with my dad, I could spot someone with a problem a mile away, but Martin wasn't exactly hiding the evidence. We moved to the futon and I looked some more around the room. There was a two-foot, half decorated Christmas tree on a TV tray near the window. This contributed to the lonely feel of the place. You could see the rest of Martin's life playing out here, and in his short trips to and from the restaurant and his work at the bookstore, where he was apparently still functioning for the time being.

Martin began telling me how handsome I was, how easy I was to talk to. He said he hadn't brought anyone home like this for a long time, which given the bleak surroundings and his obvious issues, might have been true. He'd already downed the vodka and now seemed very drunk, as he began to grope and tug at me, crawling all over me in fact. His breath was terrible and his movements were jumpy and awkward. Luckily, because of the state he was in, he wasn't up to much and I let my mind wander through the rest of it.

I woke up at dawn, the soft winter light streaming through the dirty windows. Martin was out cold. I crossed to the bathroom. I'd made it through the night and now wanted to get out of there as soon as possible, before Martin woke up, before he got any ideas about us hooking up again. It was ugly and depressing there. I'd have to think up another plan for the next evening. I put my clothes on as quietly as I could and went to leave. The gift box was sitting on a chair near the front door. I hadn't noticed it earlier, but I knew what it was before I lifted its lid. I looked over at Martin, drooling and unzipped on the futon and thought, quite simply, that he didn't deserve that cash. He'd only drink it up, I told myself. He'd squander it the way my father had squandered all his paychecks and everything else in his life. At least, if I took it, I'd be putting it to practical use—by which I meant my own survival. I barely hesitated before reaching in and scooping up the bills. I didn't count them until I was out in the hallway: $1200. I wasn't worried too much about getting caught. The only thing Martin really knew about me was my work at the answering service, but I hadn't told him which one (there were a ton of these places) and I wasn't even working there anymore. Plus, he didn't have my actual name. I doubted Martin would go to the police. He was a careless drunk who'd been ripped off by a gay hustler. (This was the only way to categorize it.) They wouldn't have given him much sympathy or attention for that. Not back then at least. Everyone would think he deserved what he got.

❖

I needn't have worried about scary silences around the dinner table. It was a talkative crowd. The food stylist, who supervised us all as we'd prepared various aspects of the citrus chicken dinner (he was particularly helpful in the juice reduction stage) told us some secrets from his time photographing food for magazine ads. Some of these I already knew—Elmer's glue in a cereal bowl, mashed potatoes for vanilla ice cream, using spray deodorant to give fruit that "cold sweat" look. He also entertained us with stories from his distant past, when he'd been a porn distributor for a time and had once been held out a 10th story window by his ankles after running afoul of the mob—a wild story, delivered with such hilarious detail, it had us all rolling. Henry sat next to Joe, and at one point he went on about some copyright issues for a book of lithographs he wanted to publish, picking my husband's brain for free legal advice. Our invitation to the island suddenly made more sense. Then the masseur told us about which celebrities had the best bodies and who had cellulite and who was well-endowed and who was not. This led to more stories about close encounters with movie stars. Martin, who was at the other end of the table (I'd sat as far away from him as possible and avoided him earlier in the bustling kitchen) told about the time he'd bumped into Tom Cruise rushing for a taxi on Fifth Avenue, literally knocking him off his feet. Joe told an appealing story I'd heard a hundred times, about striking up a conversation with Molly Ringwald, as she stood behind him in the checkout line at a Food Emporium. Then, after that, Joe turned to me and told me I should mention the celebrities I'd spoken with at the answering service. I thought I felt Martin turn his gaze in my direction, some heightened interest, but I was careful to avoid any eye contact and couldn't really be sure. The food stylist didn't wait for me to respond. He was already laughing, mentioning a Ryan Gosling lookalike at his steam room and then the conversation took on another tone entirely.

❖

"You were quiet tonight," Joe said.
Dinner was over and so was the cleanup. Now we were in our

room, getting ready for bed. The room was large and comfortable, with Hockney prints on the cream-colored walls and an ivory duvet covering the king-sized bed.

"Was I?" I said. "Tough competition, I guess. Lose your breath, you lose your turn."

"Rare for you to be so quiet," Joe replied, with his trademark concern.

"Are you going to be able to help Henry?" I asked, changing the subject.

"I don't know. I told him to send me the documents on Monday."

"Well, now we know why we got invited."

"Hey look, he could have just called me on the phone, Nate. At least we're getting a weekend out of it."

My husband's upbeat spin was something I'd come to count on through the years.

"True," I said and then Joe kissed me goodnight and turned out the lamp beside the bed.

❖

When I'd left Martin's place that morning it was still very early, but I figured I should walk in the direction of Port Authority and pick up my stuff. Then maybe I'd find a cheap hotel, some place with a weekly rate. I was going to have to be careful with expenses, but at least I wasn't panicked anymore. I kept touching the cash in my pocket. When I was just past Washington Square Park I saw one of the operators from the answering service coming toward me on the sidewalk. We greeted each other warmly (two early morning wanderers) though we barely spoke to each other at work. I'm not even sure if he knew I'd been fired. He was a straight guy named Finch who mostly kept to himself. Now on the street he was telling me he was quitting the service and moving to London. He was leaving his bombed out apartment in the East Village where he lived with three other guys. His spot there was up for grabs and so I took it, moving in right away.

Later one of these roommates would recommend me as a server for his brother's catering company in Chelsea, doing deliveries, cleaning the kitchen, working my way up. A couple of months into the job I had to go to a law firm in midtown where I was shown into a conference room. I had to unpack sandwiches and put everything on a table for a luncheon. I lost my grip on a coffee urn and the coffee spilled everywhere. The office manager and one of the secretaries kept screaming at me while I was down on the carpet trying to soak up the spill with napkins. A good-looking associate (whose parents owned a sandwich shop, as it turned out) came barreling in with paper towels from the men's room. He kneeled down next to me and helped me clean up the mess as we traded shy smiles. This, of course, was Joe.

His reflexive kindness that day got my attention. It was something I wasn't used to. And then, once we started going out (he'd come back to the conference room later and written his phone number on my wrist, a movie gesture, when I was packing everything up) he watched me with such determined optimism; it was as if he was willing some better version of me to the surface. It took me a while to realize this was how Joe watched everyone, how he basically looked at the whole world and me in particular. This knowledge only seemed to make him more irresistible. I did try to become a better person, more or less. I worked hard to justify Joe's blind faith in me anyway. Meeting Joe was like being caught up in the current of a river. This was one way to explain it, as corny as it sounds. I was swept along anyway—into marriage and parenthood and to the suburbs, happily for the most part, if you don't count that affair and a few other petty, stupid complaints.

I couldn't sleep, so I got up, threw on some shorts and a T-shirt and walked quietly through the beach house. I took the spiral staircase up to the roof deck. There was a party going on next door, at the home of the beautiful boys, music flooding through the speakers and a surge of laughter echoing in the darkness. I stood watching the summer sky which was mostly overcast that night. The ocean rippled like a black sheet in the distance.

I didn't notice him right away. Then I was aware of some movement to my left. He was sitting in one of the Adirondack chairs. I saw the ember of the cigarette he was holding first, glowing red in the dark. Henry had signs up all over the place—*If you're smoking, you had better be on fire*, so Martin was flouting the rule and taking a chance.

"I'm sorry," I said. "I didn't know anyone was up here."

"I didn't mean to startle you," Martin replied.

He put the cigarette out then, got up and walked over to me.

"It's you. Isn't it?"

I didn't say anything. I kept staring out toward the ocean.

"I had an inkling," he continued. "But I wasn't sure until tonight when Joe mentioned the answering service. Do you mind me saying I would never have recognized you?"

"I've changed, I guess."

"Yes, you have. A lot. You were very handsome once."

"I remember you though," I said.

"Do you? Do you now?"

"Yes."

We stood there for a minute without saying anything else. Whitney Houston's *I Get So Emotional* was playing next door, loud and jubilant, as if it was still the 80s.

"You didn't ruin my life or anything, Nate," Martin said now. "Or should I say Caleb?"

"I'm glad to hear it," I said, "that I didn't ruin your life."

"You weren't important enough to do that. You weren't even important enough to get me sober. It took another three years and more messed up behavior for that to happen."

He chuckled tiredly.

I didn't know what to say. An apology didn't seem to be what he was after. And I wasn't sure I could pull off the sincerity of it anyway.

"I assume Joe doesn't know. No worries there. This isn't a blackmail thing. I won't tell him or Henry either for that matter, though I think Henry's heard the story before, in our 12-step meetings, when I've shared how some hustler ripped me off one Christmas while my mother was dying."

I stayed silent as Martin moved toward the stairs.

"I wouldn't mind getting the $1200 back," he said, without turning around to look at me. "It might be a way you can exercise a little generosity of spirit, something you didn't possess in your youth. But it will have to be up to you. You know where to find me. You could come to the store. Good night, Nate."

And then he was gone.

I stayed on the roof deck. It was quieter now across the way. The party was either winding down or had moved inside. I believed Martin when he said he wouldn't tell Joe. I assumed this was somehow tied in with his sobriety and his 12-step work, some notion of personal forgiveness I couldn't quite wrap my head around. He certainly could have been crueler to me or angrier, something beyond telling me I had aged badly. I might not even have to give back the $1200. I'd have to think about that part.

Before I went downstairs and crawled back into bed with Joe, I remembered something from years before, back when my affair had ended with that dad from Ellie's school. I hadn't been the one to end it. Whenever I tried to, it didn't take. I referred to our frequent reconciliations as relapses, not always in jest. I didn't love this guy. It was more like a pigheaded yearning, a mulish lust. We'd been taking more and more risks as the affair went on. It was only a matter of time before we'd be found out and then I'd be exposed as the fraud that I was—a faithless husband; a languid, selfish parent. How my mindless narcissism might have done us all in. Then this man, my lover, had come to me with the news that he was taking a job in North Carolina; mostly to get away from me. He was moving there with his family. His wife was pregnant again. I remember conjuring a reaction of grief and distress when he told me he was leaving, but the truth was that I was filled with nothing but relief, because it had all been taken out of my hands. It felt like the other lucky times in my life, when suddenly, out of nowhere, I'd been saved.

HE HAD NO CHOICE

Alison R. Solomon

"He had no choice," you explain to our guests who are sipping mimosas and dipping their homemade focaccia into olive oil. "David had to leave."

Here we go, I think. You're going to tell my story. I should stop you, say that I don't want to be the center of attention and that anyway, you have it all wrong. Can't we discuss my dissertation instead? But I know your lover's personal history is much more interesting to the guys seated at our dining table than any academic subject. I stay silent and watch you sweep your hair back from your forehead with your fingers to stop it falling over your brow. I feel a mixture of fondness and irritation.

"Tell us!" our guests clamor.

"You okay with that?" you ask me.

I nod, even though I know I'll end up feeling like one of those caged toucans we saw on display in the Costa Maya cruise port, a captive creature, unfamiliar and exotic.

"His parents wanted him to get married," you say.

A collective sigh reverberates around the table.

"Don't they all!" Donte rolls his eyes dramatically, shaking his head.

"But it was different in his case," you say, pausing for effect. "It was an *arranged* marriage."

Our guests, Johnathan and Donte, Doug and his latest boy-toy pause in their actions. Donte's wineglass is suspended mid-air,

Johnathan's focaccia forgotten, as they turn their heads from one end of the hewn-oak table to the other and look at me.

"He was eighteen and—"

"Eighteen?" Donte screeches, turning to me. "You were just a child. Who gets married at eighteen?"

I feel my stomach muscles tighten, hearing the judgment, as I've heard it so many times before.

"In my community, kids don't date," I say. "We don't kiss or make-out or hold hands. Boys aren't even allowed to look at girls. But we were still like any other horny teenagers, so trust me, by eighteen we're more than ready to get married!"

This is the pattern. I make a joke of it. Lighten the mood. Let the story unfold as if it doesn't break me apart a little bit more each time.

"They took him to meet a girl," you continue. "His parents were in the living room and they sat in the kitchen."

"What was she like?"

"Was she pretty?"

"Were you going to go through with it?"

They fire questions at me, and I feel as if I'm transitioning from a caged toucan to a captured revolutionary.

"I didn't look at her. I kept my head down while she served me a cup of lemon tea and rugelach she'd baked that afternoon."

"Oh, I love rugelach," Johnathan says. "Definitely worth marrying a woman if her rugelach are good enough!" The group erupts in laughter as Donte punches his husband lightly on the arm.

"So then what happened?"

"We sat in silence for a while. She was waiting for me to open up the conversation, but I didn't know what to say."

I pick up the dish of butternut squash and kale strata and push it toward Donte, intimating that everyone should carry on with their meals. As they pass the dish between them, I breathe in the heady, sweet scents from the lilies and roses I cut from our garden this morning, now arranged in a Venetian glass vase on the sideboard. I love this house you and I have built together with its massive oak beams and natural light streaming in through large, uncovered windows. I relish waking to the sound of rain dripping off the trees and watching the early morning fog rise off the mountains. I want to stay in this place, not go back to the boy who lived in a Hasidic Brooklyn neighborhood, on the day he sat nervously at a peeling Formica kitchen table, shockeling back and forth, like a boy on the spectrum rocking or me reciting my thrice-daily prayers.

"Did you marry her?" asks Doug, quietly, stirring me from my reverie. Doug grew up Mennonite and I often feel an affinity with him, even though our backgrounds are so disparate.

I shake my head. "I considered it. After the first meeting, her parents told my parents she was willing to meet with me again. I thought about how nice it would be to have kids of my own, to teach them all our traditions, to be a father."

"But you're gay! How could you even contemplate it?" Doug's boy-toy looks indignant and Doug pats his leg indulgently.

"I knew plenty of guys who got married even though I was pretty sure they were gay too. None of us said anything of course. Jerking each other off at *yeshiva* was commonplace, and you had a feeling who was doing it just for himself and who had something else going on. My best friend had just got engaged and I thought I would too."

The boy-toy shakes his head. "That's just wrong," he mutters, and I want to slap his pretty little face.

I remember the second meeting with Gita. We went to a café, sitting carefully in public where her aunt, watching from a nearby table, could keep an eye on us. I ordered drinks and Gita laughed when the froth from the cappuccino lingered on my barely formed mustache. She was nice, and as I peered up at her I thought perhaps I could go through with it after all.

"So then what happened?" Donte asks.

I'm silent as I let you take up your version of my story.

"He got together with her again—with the family spying on them of course—even though he knew perfectly well he wasn't going to go through with it."

I didn't know that. I was earnest in wanting to make it work. I let you continue talking while I picture what actually happened.

"What do you want from marriage?" I asked her.

"Children," she said, as if it were the most obvious thing in the world.

"God-willing," I responded, thinking that if we focused on the children, we could make it work. "What else?"

"To have a relationship where we can share a mutual respect."

I liked that. She didn't use the word love. Maybe she didn't expect romance, just to be treated well. I could do that.

"Is there anything that would be a dealbreaker?" I asked.

She paused then said, "My mameh used to be secular. Did you know that? Does it matter to you?"

I didn't mind at all. If her mother didn't grow up orthodox, maybe it meant they were more open-minded than other families.

"If our parents and the shadchan think we're suited, then your mameh must have passed inspection," I said, and we both smiled. I felt happy. It was all going to work out. I didn't know how I'd manage the other part of me, but for now this was good.

"What stopped you from going through with it, Dave?" Doug asks, bringing me out of my reverie.

I know what they want me to say. That I had to be true to who I really was; that I was ready to abandon my community in order to live an authentic life. But it wasn't that simple, and I still haven't told anyone the way it really happened. I should have told you when we first got together, but I thought you might abandon me, and I needed you. I let you continue the story.

"How was he going to marry a girl?" you say. "He knew he was gay. Eventually, he told his parents why he couldn't do it and they told him he had to leave."

"Leave their house?" asks Donte, pulling on one of his dreads. The movement reminds me of how I used to twirl the side curls I wore all my life. It was soothing, like a child sucking his thumb. I wear my hair cropped short now and I miss it.

Doug butts in.

"Leave the community," he says authoritatively. "You know, like being excommunicated, right?"

They all look at me, so I nod.

"You're better off without them," boy-toy says emphatically. I put down my bread knife, so I won't be tempted to stab him with it. What does he know?

"He gave up his whole way of life," you tell them. "Stopped eating kosher, keeping the sabbath, praying three times a day."

You don't know that I haven't given up praying. I do it silently or when you're not around. At dusk I find myself reciting the beautiful

Maariv Aravim prayer, thanking a God I don't think I believe in for setting the stars in the sky. At night, when I can't sleep, I cling to the words of the *Shema*, as comforting and familiar as a baby's blanket.

"But Dave, how on earth did you know where to go?" Johnathan asks.

You answer for me. "To me, of course! I'd met him the previous year, stayed in his home for a couple of days. It was an anthropology thing. I asked to stay with an ultra-orthodox family to learn more about them and his family obliged. It was eye-opening, the way they lived. Like medieval Europe. David was at yeshiva during the day but when he came home and took off his big hat, I noticed his eyes right away. I watched how he moved and wondered about him, but he never paid any attention to me. I gave him my phone number on a whim, just in case he ever made it out of there."

You make it sound like a prison and that I was lucky to escape. It was a cocoon, warm, nurturing, and safe. When a butterfly emerges from its chrysalis, its wings are small and wet, and it can't yet fly. Your number was the only thing I had that was going to teach me how to enter this new world. I had no idea I would fall in love with you.

"What's going on, Dave?" Doug eyes me intently. "Is there something you're not saying? You seem as if you're miles away."

"Thinking about how glad you are to be out of that backwards society, I'll bet," says boy-toy, and this time I can't stop myself.

"No!" I bang the table, the way my father did when I begged to stay.

Everyone turns to stare at me and for a moment I hesitate. I'm so tired of people presuming they know how I feel, but if I never tell them the truth, what can I expect? I don't tell you and others how I really feel because I think you'll despise me. Who would mourn a community that doesn't accept them? Who would feel the loss of rules and rituals that make no logical sense? I've spent a lifetime feeling insecure and it wears me down. I open my mouth before I can change my mind.

"There are things about my former life I miss so badly I feel as if part of my heart was ripped out when I left. I didn't call Ozzie because I was into him. I called him because I had no one else to turn to." I turn and face you. "I'm sorry," I say, my voice low and quiet.

You look at me, your eyes filled with hurt.

"I'm tired of holding onto secrets. I want you to know what really happened," I say, without stopping to think whether I'm ready to do this. "I wasn't some superhero, ready to abandon everything for love. I was going to go through with the marriage. My parents and I went to see Gita's parents to tell them I was ready to be engaged. When we got there, a boy my own age answered the door. Even though he looked just like all of us—his hair covered with a big, black yarmulka, his tzitzis hanging from his shirt—I felt my whole body start to shake. I wanted to leap on top of him, grab his face, force my tongue into those soft lips that smiled between his half-grown mustache. I went rock hard and had to stop myself from grabbing my crotch to cover it. Gita's parents came up from behind him and said, 'Ah, so you've met Hershel, Gita's brother. He just got married and we bought a duplex so he and his bride can have one side and Gita and her husband the other.'"

Reboyne shel oylem! He would be my neighbor. I would see him every day. It would be exhilarating. Terrifying. Disastrous.

"So what did you do?" Johnathon asks.

"I wish I could tell you that I realized living next door to Hershel would be torture and that I found a way to wriggle out of the marriage tactfully. But I didn't. What actually happened is that my heart was palpitating so hard, I guess I forgot to breathe. I fainted. When I came to, someone was cradling my head and without thinking, I said, 'Hershel?' and reached up and stroked his face. It was Gita's father who was holding me. My family and I never made it past the hallway. My mother tried to placate everyone and say I was confused and didn't know what I was doing. She said I thought it was Gita but that I just said Hershel because he was the last person I'd seen before I fainted. But my father and Gita's father knew right away what was going on."

"You have to admit it's romantic," Johnathan says. "Fainting from love. Did you ever get to see Hershel again?"

"No. I left pretty soon after that. My parents and I had a long talk. They said there was no point in trying to marry me off because what had happened was going to be all over Brooklyn the next day which meant that by the day after it would be in every corner of the community, from Hendon in England to Bnei Brak in Israel. They told me I should go into the secular world and make a life for myself."

I sip water while I replay the scene in my head.

"Let me stay, Mameh," I begged, after Tateh banged on the table and made his decree. I knew it hurt him to do it. Mameh's eyes were red from crying. Even Tateh had tears in his eyes.

"We're doing this for you, kindele. If you stay here, you have to live our life. You'd have to have a wife, but we won't be able to find you one. Without that, you won't be invited to shabbes dinners, maybe not even to weddings and simchas. You'll be an outcast."

"But if I leave, I can still come home for shabbes dinner? And see Dinah and Moishe, right?"

"So that you can watch them making lives you can never have? It will tear you apart. You'll be better off creating a new life for yourself."

"How do you know that?" I wasn't thinking about finding a man to love, just about the idea of never going to my schul again, never sitting at the shabbes table, swaying from side to side as we all sang songs together, the melodies making my heart soar, even while the heavy cholent weighed down my stomach. I was thinking about Mameh being bubbie to my children, and me being an uncle to Dinah's future children.

"Let me tell you a secret," Mameh said, stroking my hair the way she hadn't since I was a child. "Remember when your cousin, Menashe, died a couple of years ago?"

I nodded, wondering why this had anything to do with anything. He'd been struck with meningitis, died within twenty-four hours.

"It wasn't meningitis. He killed himself."

I stared at her wide-eyed and bewildered. "But he had a funeral. They wouldn't have given him a funeral if he killed himself. It's against halacha."

"Yes, but only his parents and your father and I know the truth. He did it with pills. Nobody had to know it wasn't meningitis. He didn't do it because he was like you but, like you, he was always going to be a pariah in our society." Mameh shuddered and I wasn't sure whether it was because of me or Menashe. "I won't tell you what he'd done, but you can trust me on this. He was trying to live in a community where he was an outcast and he couldn't do it." She sighed and leaned toward me. "We'll find a way to stay in touch, but you can't stay here."

I heave a sigh and Doug turns to me. "So you left the only world you ever knew. Were you okay with that, Dave?"

How could I be okay when my world was shattering and crashing around me and all I could see was the debris left behind?

Everyone's looking at me and I realize I need to answer.

"It was a loss," I say, my vocal cords straining to work through the lump forming in my throat.

"But once you'd been in the real world for a while, you must have realized everything you'd gained, right?" Donte says. "You went to university and got an education. You have this house and most importantly, you have Ozzie."

I grimace. People always think I must be better off in this secular world, where I can have everything I want, except maybe the one thing I want most of all, my family.

"You lost your community," Doug says quietly. "I know how tough that can be. But look at it this way: you got all of us, a new community to replace the old one. We're your family now."

I feel a stab of pain. He's right, even though he's not.

"And you can never lose being Jewish," says Johnathan. "You should come to our temple. It's totally welcoming to the queer community and the woman rabbi is adorable. You'd love it."

There is so much about this statement that I could refute. The very word temple makes me shudder as if Johnathan had used the word church to describe a Jewish place of worship. Jews have schuls or synagogues—our holy temples were destroyed centuries ago. As for his woman rabbi, while my logical mind knows it's the right thing that in this world women can be religious leaders, my heart hasn't caught up with that idea yet.

"Do you guys mind if I don't talk about this anymore?" I say and then, before I can stop myself, I burst into tears.

Boy-toy looks acutely embarrassed but the other three immediately jump up to hand me tissues, rub my shoulders, give me water. They circle around, Doug and Donte crouching on either side. Warmth and comfort flow from them as they murmur apologies and support. The gestures are so soothing that I remind myself I do have a family, just not the one I was born into.

I look down to the other end of the table where you sit, watching me, your eyes wary. Have I lost you?

"I'm sorry," I say. "I should have told you. At the beginning, I needed you so much, I was scared to admit how it all went down. Then it felt like too much time had passed to tell you something that should have been said from the start. I'll understand if you feel you can't trust me anymore. I've never told you because I didn't want to risk losing you, but I've lost everything once. I can deal with going through it again."

You pull yourself slowly out of your chair, shaking your head. "That's not it," you say. You come over and kneel in front of me, your hands clasping mine.

"Are there any other secrets you've kept?" you ask.

"Sometimes I feel as if everyone thinks that our life is so wonderful, I shouldn't care about what happened to me. People think I should be angry at my parents and my community. But all I feel is the loss, the pain, the emptiness. I've let go of everything material about it, but I haven't let go of it in my heart."

"Oh, sweetie, you don't have to. I thought you wanted a clean break, but if there are things you need to take back, tell me. You want to keep shabbat—shabbes as you would say—we can do that. You want to stop eating shrimp, I won't bring it home anymore."

I shake my head in wonder. "You're so good to me," I say. "Maybe you really were my *bashert*, the one I was destined for."

"Is there anything we can do to help?" Doug asks.

Nobody's ever asked me this before. Is there something they can do? I've always considered my struggle an internal thing, something only I can figure out, without involving others. Before I left home, I never confided in anyone. Moishe would have had no idea what to say and Dinah had been too young to talk to. I did consider talking to Mameh, but my courage always deserted me. The feeling I had a few moments ago was that these men, along with our other friends, are now my chosen family. Maybe I can do things differently with this family.

But how can they help? I long so much for what I don't have, for my old community, for shabbes, for connection with Hashem, that I feel as if I'm still in mourning. Is there any way they can help me move forward, into a new future, while not totally closing the door on my past? Before my brain can start sifting through ideas, my heart gives me an answer. Ever since I left my community, people have botched my name. First, they anglicized it to David. Then they shortened it to Dave. Even guys like Johnathan, who think they're saying it right when they use a Hebrew pronunciation, emphasizing the second syllable instead of the first, have it wrong. It's got to the point where I've stopped trying to use my real name even though I cringe every time they use their monikers. I know I have to build my new way of life, but I guess I have to accept that there are some parts I can't let go.

"There is one thing you can do," I say softly, looking around the room at this group of men that has become so dear to me. "My name is Dovid. You can start by calling me Dovid."

"We can do that, Dovid," you say, with perfect pronunciation. You stand up and shake out your legs, cramped from kneeling in front of me. "Why today, Dovid? What happened that you decided to tell us the whole truth?"

I look at you, seeing the acceptance in your eyes, feeling the warmth of your presence.

"I had no choice," I say.

Two Sides

Carrie Smith

Tamisha was winning again, but I didn't care. I just wanted to keep the game going as long as I could, our bodies hunched forward and our faces so close I could feel the slight current of her breath between us as we studied the board. It was her move again, and she took her time, playing out the consequences, seeing more of the future than I ever could.

Finally she sat up tall and resolute. I followed her hand to the board. Her thumb and forefinger delicately lifted a knight, held it in the air, and set it down again. "Check."

I wanted those fingers to reach out to me. Did she know it? Did she feel that too?

I was in the tenth grade at a private high school that according to my father cost "a pretty penny" but would save me from being bussed to the inner city if Milliken v. Bradley made its way to the Supreme Court and the justices made the "wrong call" on cross-district integration.

He and my mother now believed I was rubbing elbows with the offspring of influential Grosse Pointe families—Fords, Chryslers, Dodges—but those kids had all learned to swing their field hockey sticks together in lower school. They didn't need any new friends like me, a middle-class kid with no pedigree. A wiffle ball player.

I felt more at ease with Tamisha, an eleventh-grade scholarship student. Every day after the last bell, we went up to the second-floor classroom where the chess club met. We were always the last to leave, fastened to our seats until the sky was ink black through the windows and the only other people up there were Miss Ferguson, the old Latin teacher, and the janitors buffing the floors.

Like Miss Ferguson, I guess, Tamisha and I had nowhere better to be.

That September my sister had left for college. My father had become an administrative law judge for worker's comp hearings, and my mother had been voted onto the local teacher's union bargaining committee, which meant she had meetings after her regular school day ended.

Every evening when we came home from our separate worlds, my father would say, "Where shall we have dinner tonight, Lo?"

My mother had given up cooking.

We usually ended up at one of three restaurants. The Elias Brothers' Big Boy on the corner of Mack and Eight Mile was the closest. In the back was an all-you-can-eat salad bar that appealed to my parents. They'd gone on Weight Watchers when my father couldn't button the slacks of his favorite suit, and one day he'd come home with a physician quality beam scale for their bedroom. "We need to weigh in every day."

Friar Tuck's in St. Clair Shores was another favorite. On the menu was a low-fat soft-serve frozen dessert that carried the Weight Watchers' seal of approval. My parents didn't seem to mind the funny aftertaste.

Bill Kavan's Bar and Grill had dim lighting and long lines, but every so often my mother craved one of their charbroiled burgers and my father would "throw caution to the wind" and order the onion rings deep fried to golden brown. I liked the BLTs made with greasy round slices of Canadian bacon.

On this Monday night my mother said, "Kavan's."

As we drove there through the November darkness, I thought of Tamisha driving home in her grandmother's beat-up Ford Falcon. Tamisha and her grandmother lived in Highland Park, far from Grosse Pointe.

"How was school?" my mother asked as we waited in line to be seated.

"Great," I said.

"You played chess again?"

I nodded.

"Who's in that chess club anyway?"

"Oh, lots of kids," I said and she didn't dig any deeper.

When we finally got to our table, my father leaned forward and told her, "Have I got some news." His eyes darted to the other tables. "John Marlon is missing."

John Marlon was one of my father's friends from Wayne State University Law School.

"Missing?" said my mother. "What do you mean, he's missing?"

My father frowned. "Keep your voice down, Lo. You never know who's listening. Let's use first initials."

"How did you find this out?" she whispered.

"L called my office this morning."

L was Linda, John Marlon's wife. Until their marriage a year ago, he'd been a "confirmed bachelor," according to my mother.

"I don't know what he sees in that girl," my father had said when their wedding invitation arrived in our mail. "She's hardly a looker."

"Oh, she's perfectly nice, Jim," said my mother. "And if you ask me, *I* don't know what *she* sees in him. He's a good fifteen years older than she is."

"I'll tell you what she sees. Dollar signs. And a rescue from Old Maid status. Either that or she's got skills we don't know about." He laughed loudly.

A Kavan's waitress set three vinyl-covered menus on the table. My father grinned up at her. "Are you our girl tonight?"

Girl? I wanted to disappear.

He read her nametag. "Cha*rise*, is it? Or *Char*ise?"

"Whichever you prefer." She didn't smile, her head cocked to one side, eyes narrowed.

My mother sat through this cringy exchange with a blank expression. My father always treated waitresses as if their job gave him license to tease and flirt. But Char*ise*—or *Char*ise—was no high-school girl like the waitresses at Big Boy. She was at least thirty and gave him a look that said *I know your type.*

"Start you off with a drink?" she asked flatly.

"Coffee for me," said my mother.

"Decaf," said my father. "Make sure it's decaf. I don't want to be up all night."

Charise turned away and my mother said, "Do you think J and L had a fight?"

"I asked her that, but she insisted everything was fine between them."

I sipped my water and sucked on little chips of crushed ice the way I'd sucked on one of Tamisha's butterscotch Lifesavers during our chess game an hour ago. As I opened my menu, I pictured John Marlon's face. His cheeks were scarred with little pock marks and the fringe of bangs across his forehead made him look like a Roman emperor. His eyes were the same blue as my grandmother's Wedgwood china. He wasn't handsome, but he was tall and striking in the expensive suits he wore to my parents' holiday parties.

Tamisha was more than striking. She had dark almond-shaped eyes, high cheekbones, and full lips that I couldn't stop staring at. She wore her hair in tight braids that almost came to her shoulders. She was beautiful, and I could look at her forever.

"L must be going crazy," said my mother.

"She's got the new baby, and she was up all night calling around."

"Did she phone the police?"

He nodded. "They wouldn't take a missing person's report until twenty-four hours elapsed. I helped her do it this afternoon."

"What do you think could have happened?"

My father rested his elbow on the table, making my water slosh. "Well, it could be related to a case," he said. "It isn't easy being an assistant prosecutor down there, you know."

Down there was Detroit.

"You're dealing with some really rough characters."

Rough characters were black people. But Tamisha wasn't rough. Her voice was soft. Her skin was smooth and creamy like rich hot cocoa.

My father scratched his five o'clock shadow with an upward flick of his nails. "Some crazy convict on parole could have wanted pay back."

I watched the waitress cross the room with two coffees.

My father looked up at her. "Are you sure this is decaf, Charise?"

"Should I swear a blood oath?" She stared at him, cup in hand.

He laughed a little too heartily to cover his embarrassment. She'd one-upped him. Good for her.

When she left, he said, "That waitress has an attitude problem."

"Go on with your story," said my mother.

My father sipped his decaf. "Well, it's also conceivable J got himself entangled in some shady business."

"What kind of business?"

"Maybe he took a bribe and didn't deliver his end of the bargain."

My mother sipped her coffee. "Really?"

My father shrugged. "Sometimes you think you know someone, Lo, only to find out they're someone else entirely. We have no idea what he was doing."

I stared into my menu. They had no idea what I was doing either.

❖

"Let's just go to the Big Boy, Jim," my mother said on Tuesday evening. "I'm tired. I want to get to bed early."

The seating hostess led us to my father's favorite section. On our way, we passed a table-for-two and it made me think of Tamisha. The two of us could come here and drink tea together. Would she want to?

Tonight, as we'd left the school, she asked me, "You want a ride home?"

"Sure," I said and walked with her across the dark parking lot.

She came to the passenger side with me and opened the door as if I were her date. I got in and she closed it for me. "Sorry for the mess," she said when she got behind the wheel. But it wasn't messy at all. Just old.

She backed out of the space as if she'd been driving forever.

I directed her to my house and she stopped at the curb to let me out. She glanced toward the front porch where a light was on. "Nice house."

It didn't seem all that nice to me. "See you tomorrow," I said, not wanting to get out.

Now my father slid into one side of the upholstered booth and my mother and I shared the other. I was on top of a section that had ripped and been repaired with packing tape. A waitress who looked about my sister's age came over with menus. My father read her nametag. "Penny. Is that by chance short for Penelope?"

She nodded.

"Are you Greek, Penelope?"

"Half Greek," she said.

"Penelope was the wife of Odysseus, the famous hero of Greek mythology. Did you know that?"

I looked out the window into the parking lot. Was he going to tell her the whole story of the suitors?

"It's a beautiful name," he said.

"Thank you." She smiled.

I wanted to tell her none of his compliments meant she was going to get a generous tip. My father never tipped well. When it came time to fill out that row on the Diners Club slip, he'd forget all about her beautiful Greek name.

Finally we ordered, Penny walked away, and he said, "I've got some news about you-know-who."

"J and L?" My mother leaned forward.

Just then Penny returned with two coffee pots—regular and decaf.

When she was out of range again, my father said, "J is still missing. I went over to the house today to be with L when a detective came to see her. Detective Smalls. He asked her lots of questions."

"What questions?"

"Had J been upset about something."

"And? Had he?"

"L claims no."

"What else did he ask?"

"Had they been fighting. And here's the interesting thing. I saw him watching her very closely. I think she may be a suspect or at least a person of interest in the case."

My mother leaned back in the booth. "You mean she might have something to do with his disappearance?"

My father's raised eyebrows suggested that she might. "If you ask me, J never should have married her. Keep in mind, they only went out a few months. He knew very little about her."

I thought about Tamisha staring at my front porch and saying, "Nice house." What kind of house did she and her grandmother live in? Where was her mother? Did she have a father? All I really knew about her was that she went to chess tournaments and was a top math student. She was taking Advanced Calculus with a small group of seniors.

"But why would L kill the father of her baby?" asked my mother.

I swiveled my head to hear my father's answer.

He tightened his lips and shrugged. "What if J had a big life insurance policy? You remember *Double Indemnity*, don't you?"

"So L is Barbara Stanwyck?"

"Bingo." He nodded. "What if all she ever wanted from him was a baby and now that she's got it, she's done with him?"

My mother scrunched up her face but said nothing.

I had another idea. What if he'd been having an affair and run off with another woman?

Penny came back with creamer for my mother's coffee.

My parents were just going to keep speculating, so I slid out of the booth and went to the salad bar. Where was Tamisha right now?

❖

On Wednesday night, my father brought Section A of the Detroit News to Friar Tuck's. We were in a spacious booth near the front of the restaurant. My father opened the paper to page three and pointed to a brief article below the fold. *Prominent Attorney Missing.*

My mother took off her glasses to read it. Finally she looked up. "They don't say anything about who did it."

Did *what?* I wondered. Was she starting to doubt my father's theory that Linda was involved?

"But if you read closely, you can glean some interesting details, Lo. For example, J left his office on Monday evening in 'good spirits.' That suggests to me that he didn't have anything weighing on his mind. That he didn't *see it coming.*"

What did he think it was? A gun shot? A knife in the back?

"Do you still think L is a suspect?" asked my mother.

"If she is, the police aren't saying."

"I just don't see her as a murderer."

"I know, but you have to remember, there are two sides to everyone."

My father was right about that. There were two sides to me. The side I showed my parents and the side that peeked out when I was with Tamisha. Tonight we'd sat in her car in the parking lot for half an hour before she drove me home. She did an impersonation of Mr. Norris, her Calculus teacher, that made us both laugh really hard, and her hand reached over and touched my arm. I don't know if she did it on purpose, but my whole chest ignited.

I wanted to ask her so many things, but I didn't want to pry. So I just said, "We should go out for tea some time" and she said she'd like that.

My mother was sipping her coffee again. "But how could L do away with him? She's no match for him physically."

"That's true, but women don't resort to brute strength when they kill. They rely on calculation. Think of Livia the Poisoner."

"Who?"

"Never mind. All I'm saying is that L could have found a way to do it if she wanted to."

"And what would she have done with the body?"

A young man appeared at our table. "Something to drink?"

My father looked up at him and squinted. Did I hear irritation in his tone when he said, "Decaf"?

No flirting tonight.

We were back at the Big Boy on Thursday, one booth over from the night before last. "They found his car," said my father as he slid in.

My mother's eyes widened. "Where?"

"Over on the west side, near Palmer Park. It had been collecting parking tickets for days. They finally ran the plates and connected it to L's missing person's report."

"But J and L lived nowhere near there."

Did Tamisha live near there? Where was Highland Park anyway?

"I know." My father combed his fingers through his black hair. "What do you make of it?"

"I'm beginning to think this *wasn't* homicide."

"Then what was it?"

"Maybe he committed *suicide*."

"*Suicide*? But why?"

My father frowned. "You just never know about people, Lo. J was always a little quirky. I think he might have been prone to depression."

"Hmmm." My mother nodded.

"Back in law school, he could be funny as hell one minute and sullen the next. I wonder if he had an undiagnosed mood disorder."

My mother nodded again, and I imagined myself back in Tamisha's car half an hour ago.

"Do your parents know you hang out with me?" she'd asked.

I knew what she meant. Did they know I had a Black friend? "I don't talk about my friends much," I said.

"But what would they say?" she asked.

I thought of all the words my father used for Black people. I felt Tamisha watching me closely, like that Detective Smalls had watched L. What would she think if she knew my parents had voted for George Wallace five years ago or that they'd put me into this private school to keep me away from people like her? Would she ever talk to me again?

I met her gaze. "I don't care what they'd say." I felt another jolt in my chest. It was hard to swallow.

A waitress flew down the aisle with four plates balanced in her arms. My father waved at her, forcing her to stop. "Are you our girl? We're hungry. We don't even have coffee yet." As if he was going to die.

She looked from him to the plates in her arms and back. "I'm so sorry. I'll drop these off and be right over. I promise."

My father turned back to my mother. "I predict they're going to find J's body in the Detroit River." I heard excitement in his voice.

"You do?" My mother's tone matched his.

Neither one of my parents sounded upset at the prospect of John Marlon's death. In fact, it seemed to make them feel more alive, the way I felt with Tamisha.

Our waitress arrived breathless and apologetic. "Can I take your order?"

On Friday night my father was running late and called to say he would meet my mother and me at a restaurant.

"I feel like something different tonight. Let's go to La Shish," I heard her tell him. My mother loved the chicken Shish Tawook and garlic spread at La Shish, even though it wasn't on her diet.

My father was already there sipping coffee when we arrived. As soon as we ordered he leaned in and told her, "I know the whole story now, Lo, and you're *not going to believe it*."

"Did they find him?"

"Yes."

"Dead or alive?"

My father held up his hand. "You remember those tickets on his car?"

She nodded. "Yes. So?"

"Guess what they found in the glove box."

"Jeez, Jim. Just tell me."

The waitress set hummus, warm pita, and garlic spread on the table.

"His wallet," said my father. "His wallet was in the glove box."

She frowned. "Why? What happened?"

"Just listen, Lo. Don't you want to know how the pieces fit together?"

"Fine." She sounded annoyed.

"He left that wallet in the car on purpose. He was going somewhere, and he didn't want anyone there to know who he was."

"Where?" she asked. "Where did he go?"

He cleared his throat. "To an establishment that caters to a certain clientele."

"What establishment?" she asked.

What clientele? I wanted to ask.

My father sipped his black decaf.

"Just tell me." My mother shook her pita triangle.

"A bathhouse."

My mother scrunched her face. "They still have those?"

I pictured the ruins of the Sutro Baths in San Francisco, where we'd vacationed two summers ago. I'd come home with a postcard of bathers in the 1890s swimming in salt-water pools under a massive glass dome.

"Not a *public* bathhouse, Lo." He sounded impatient, as if she were an idiot. "I'm talking about a bathhouse frequented by *ho-mo-sex-u-als*."

My mother's mouth formed a silent O of understanding. I froze. I didn't even breathe.

"The police showed his driver's license photo to businesses in the area and it turns out he went into one of those places."

"And someone killed him there?"

"No. He had a heart attack." He gave her a knowing look. "You know. Like your father. Only different."

She glared back at him. "I told you never to mention that again."

He raised his hand in a *calm down* gesture.

I knew what they were talking about. Last summer my sister had learned the details of our grandfather's death while she'd played receptionist in our father's law office. Three years before I was born, our grandfather had suffered a heart attack while having sex with a prostitute at a hotel in Detroit. And not just any prostitute. A *Black* prostitute. This was my mother's unspoken shame.

My father had a weird smile. "No wonder J left his office in 'good spirits' on Monday."

My mother shook her head slowly, lips compressed into disapproval.

"His body's been lying in the city morgue all this time."

I watched my mother's upper lip curl.

"I always knew there was something off about him," said my father.

"You did?"

"You know how men are when they get together and joke. But J never had much to say when the topic of women came around."

"But you liked him," said my mother.

"Well, he could be very witty and sarcastic. Bitter, now that I think of it. Which makes sense. Those men tend to be that way, you know."

Those men? That way?

"He was leading a double life, Lo. He fooled us. He fooled all of us. Even his wife. What kind of person can do that?"

I swiveled my head in time to watch my mother say, "A sicko. A *real sicko.*" Disgust dripped from her voice.

My father sipped his decaf.

I remembered sitting in Tamisha's Ford Falcon an hour ago, parked two blocks from my house, hidden by the night, our knees touching. "I wish I didn't have to go home."

"I wish you didn't either," she said.

Her hand reached for my hand. It was so warm.

She leaned forward and kissed me. Her lower lip was a little chapped and she tasted like a butterscotch Lifesaver. I kissed her back. I felt so alive in that kiss.

What did that make me?

LUCKY BASTARD

William Christy Smith

Just as he slid the key into the door lock, it dawned on Clay that he should have informed his roommate last week that he was going away for the weekend. Of course, it might have been intentional to have skipped this detail.

When he gently swung the door open, a newspaper rustled, probably one that Lily, his roommate and old high school pal, was reading. It occurred to him that she might be rolling it up to hit him.

"Clay Byrd, where have you been?" Lily lowered the paper and was looking over it with a scowl on her face.

"Nowhere," he said. "Just out." He made it sound as if he had gone down to the corner market to snag a candy bar.

"All weekend?" she asked. "How does that happen? I can't tell you how many people I called trying to track you down."

She'd been lying on the couch but had risen when Clay entered the room. She was wearing a black muumuu with purple, green and red trim that made her look bigger than she was, though she would be considered a "big girl" by most. Clay surmised that she hadn't been out of the apartment all day, but her make-up had been applied and hair pulled back. She'd been a beauty queen in her youth but had never advanced far because of her Rubenesque physique. She was still attractive with smooth, unblemished skin and deep brown eyes, but more often than not, she wore a look of disappointment on her face.

Clay had known he'd be grilled on his whereabouts. He knew she'd disapprove.

"I went to a seminar in Baton Rouge," he confessed, and rubbed the top of his head, like someone who'd bumped into a sign.

"That Louise Hay seminar you told me you weren't going to?" she asked, but it was more of a statement than a question. Her eyes had closed into horizontal slits.

Clay and Lily had been through many arguments about Louise Hay and her self-help techniques. Lily thought Hay's theories that positive thinking could heal disease were dangerous and fraudulent. She didn't care if they were sweeping the country or not. Clay wanted to believe Louise Hay was a godsend. She had a big following among gay men who'd turned to her holistic strategies to fight HIV.

"No harm in checking it out," he said. He felt like a child who'd been caught stealing candy from the drug store. "I went with some of the guys from the writers' group that meets at the restaurant."

"Oh, Clay." She sighed. "Why are you wasting money on that nonsense? It's just a rip-off."

"That's your opinion," Clay murmured. A negative thought, he told himself. He closed his eyes and visualized himself writing Lily's comments on a piece of toilet paper and flushing it down the toilet. "This past weekend has been something important for me. I feel changed."

"How so?" Contempt filled her voice.

"Well, I learned that I can improve my own health by being gentle and kind and patient." He pointed his nose at Lily when he said this.

"What else did you learn?" Lily asked.

Clay sighed. "I learned that I need to stop criticizing myself and others because criticism never solves a thing," he said, hoping she couldn't miss his message. "I learned that I need to forgive myself and let the past go."

"You had to go to an expensive seminar ninety miles away to learn that? I could have told you for free."

He shot her a wicked side glance. She just couldn't see what he'd experienced. How could she? She was as jaded as he'd been, hadn't learned yet how to love herself, as he was learning to do.

"Lily," he said. "I just want to try and live a more truthful life. I want to be more honest, and I need to grow up."

She maintained a blank stare. Was she beginning to understand or was she just indulging him? For a minute, he wondered if she was going to dismiss the conversation and return to her newspaper. He wanted to tell her about the workshops—how to lovingly release old negative patterns, how to praise yourself and to avoid criticism that breaks down the inner spirit, how to look into the mirror and express the love one has for oneself.

He also wanted to tell her about that seminar on nutrition and wellness, and how he intended to create a plan that would bring him back to optimum health. But not right now. He was tired and she wasn't ready. She was too negative.

"So, Mister Honesty," she said. "In this new life of yours do you plan to tell your dad that you and I are merely roommates and not the heterosexual couple he thinks we are?"

He paused. "Yes, I intend to do that."

"And do you also plan to tell him that you're gay?"

"Yes, I'll do that too."

"And do you also plan to tell your father that you happen to be HIV-positive?"

Clay sighed. "I plan to tell him everything."

"Do you think you'll do it this upcoming weekend?"

"Why do I have to do it this weekend?"

"Because while you were away on your little Louise Hay Ride, your dad called several times and wanted to speak to you. He wants you to come home next weekend. He was very insistent."

Clay sucked in a gulp of air, then blew it out slowly. He hadn't planned on becoming so honest this quickly.

The average person had anywhere from sixty to one hundred heartbeats per minute. That was one of the things Clay had learned during the past weekend. He also learned that the average person had about eighty thousand thoughts per day, and of these, about eighty percent were negative or nonproductive, or they were repetitive or not helpful. The goal was to identify the negative thoughts and reprogram them into positive thoughts.

At that moment, Clay felt as if the statistics had to be underestimated. His heart was beating a mile a minute and his mind was filled with horrible thoughts of a trip home. He retreated to his bedroom, shut the door, and tried to collect himself by unpacking the small bag he'd taken to Baton Rouge. He took his time, trying to figure out what his dad wanted now.

Clay decided to burn some sage to clear the negativity. Then he rolled his neck from side to side, then took in a deep breath and exhaled slowly, just like the exercises the men had performed at the seminar in Baton Rouge. He did this several times, then planted himself in front of the mirror.

"You *are* a person of worth," he whispered. "You *are* smart and resourceful, and you can get through this."

He turned his face to the side and checked his image in profile, then rotated to the other side of his face. Were those bags under his eyes? Was he aging gracefully?

Clay had been a handsome man in a lazy way. His face was more arresting than beautiful, his expressions pitying and a little sorrowful, as if he was viewing with resignation the whole enterprise of living. He was five foot eight sober, with dishwater blond hair that was beginning to sprout some grey, a small button nose, and sad blue eyes. He wasn't a frail person but that was the idea he sometimes conveyed, tired at the ripe old age of thirty-four.

He had spent a great deal of his twenties in pursuit of erotic congress. It took the Mississippi country boy a little time to get started, but once he began, he became a fan for life, a practiced hand at nocturnal ramblings. Lily never approved and said his romantic entanglements lasted, on average, about forty-five minutes. It wasn't that she was opposed to him having lovers, just that the turnover rate was too high in her estimation. She'd identified several men that she found suitable for Clay, but he hadn't been interested in settling down.

His diagnosis didn't slow him down much. He knew plenty of guys now sharing the same boat he was in. He developed a new philosophy for his new lifestyle: *You don't have to stop living just because you know you are going to die.* No one appreciated the stamina of the hedonist.

The one stable factor in his life was his job. He was the senior photographer at Charity Hospital, documenting everything from employees of the month, to autopsies. His experiences shooting the cadavers of those who had died prolonged deaths from various diseases formed the root of his doubt about traditional medical practices.

"These patients, they get poked and prodded, and they don't know what's happening to them, and the doctors do whatever they want," he explained to Lily. "It's a horrible end. I don't want to die like that. I want to take charge of my own health."

He knew she wasn't listening, but she'd been with him through everything, and it didn't seem to him that she was going anywhere. She definitely hadn't understood the tarot cards he'd worked so hard to understand, and she said the incense made her nauseous. She was equally unimpressed with the ritual he'd planned to cleanse some rocks and minerals—jade, hematite, pyrite and pink quartz in the glow of the full moon. He'd carefully washed the stones and placed them in a row on the balcony ledge to charge them to their potential. She'd stepped out onto the balcony and discovered them.

"What pretty stones," she'd said. She picked up each one to examine it, not realizing that her touch would negate any power Clay would derive. He half-heartedly blamed her for the bad luck he experienced the next day—a roll of film that contained underexposed images of a new x-ray machine that was needed by the hospital public relations department.

"You're not serious, are you?" Lily defended herself, a look of astonishment on her face.

He just shook his head back and forth in a noncommittal shrug.

"Clayton Robert Byrd," she practically shouted. "We need to firmly grasp reality by the hand, don't we?"

He'd kept his rocks and minerals in his room after that incident.

❖

"Clay, what are you doing in there?" Lily yelled. "Get out here and call your dad before he calls again."

He sighed again, closed his eyes, exhaled, then inhaled. "Yes, you are a person of worth, even though you might feel you are surrounded by fools."

Then he mouthed into the air, "Sorry for the negativity."

He rejoined Lily, who had remained firmly planted on the couch in her muumuu, except that she had traded the newspaper for a paperback.

"If you don't call him today, you know what he'll say?" she scolded. Then she imitated the older man. "'Why didn't you call on Sunday? It's cheaper.' You know what a cheapskate your dad is."

She sat up on the couch, giving Clay half to sit on.

"He's not going to mellow, is he?" Clay said.

"He's not a fine wine."

"I'm not really looking forward to this," Clay said.

"I don't blame you."

They sat in silence for a while as the day turned pale, then shadowed and died.

Time grew thick as molasses, then thin as turpentine when Lily pointedly asked Clay how long he thought he could stall.

"Lily," Clay said. "You may not know this, but I am a flawed person."

She laughed and ended up choking on her Diet Dr Pepper.

❖

At eight o'clock on Sunday night, a full hour after rates went down for long distance telephone calls, Clay mouthed an affirmation and dialed the number of the home where he'd been raised, an American Craftsman house in Bluebonnet, Mississippi, population 435, located forty miles from the border with Louisiana and six miles from the Mighty Mississippi River.

"Dad, hello, it's Clay." He spent the next ninety seconds explaining how he had gone to a seminar in Baton Rouge but hadn't bothered to take his fiancée.

"When are you going to marry that girl?" his father asked. "Remember that family tree of ours. You're the only one to keep it going."

More like a family shrub than a family tree, Clay thought, but he kept his opinions to himself. Judge Armand Louis Byrd was not much of a conversationalist and frequently stuck to a handful of tried-and-true topics rather than venture into unexplored territory. Predictable, he had a strict moral code for those around him. He was quiet and taciturn and told people he wore his heart on the inside, where it belonged.

"Well," Clay stalled. "Perhaps we can talk about that later. I heard that you wanted me to come home next weekend. Is there something wrong?"

"No, but there's something interesting happening that came up, and it involves our family. There's a big to-do at the courthouse, and the mayor and other city officials are going to open a time capsule from seventy years ago, from 1918. It's probably just a box of junk but it might be interesting. I know there's a letter in it from your great-great-uncle Thomas, who was a soldier in World War I, to a friend who grew up here named Jack Stansfield. This Stansfield guy never came back and the letter was never opened. Apparently, he didn't have any family, and no one knew what to do with the letter, so they put it into the time capsule. They're going to open it and read it."

Clay admitted to himself that the opening of a time capsule was appealing, but the thought of spending an entire weekend in the town of his youth didn't thrill him. "I'll come up on Saturday morning, if that's okay."

"Why don't you come up on Friday evening, son." His father's tone was more serious now. "I have some other things I want to tell you."

"There're some things I want to tell you too." Clay was surprised to hear himself say these words.

"Great. I'll see you this Friday night."

Clay put the phone back into the receiver and without looking at Lily, returned to the bathroom and looked at himself in the mirror, focusing on his eyes.

"You can do this," he coached himself. "You can change and become kinder and more balanced. You can be more honest to yourself and to others. Your father won't be happy, but in the long run, he'll understand. You'll come back a better person."

Then he realized his breathing had become extremely difficult, so labored that he wondered if he was having a panic attack. He flushed the toilet so Lily couldn't hear.

On Friday afternoon, Clay repacked the bag he'd taken to the Louise Hay seminar. He made it to the front door but stopped when he saw Lily perched on the couch, pretending to read a beauty magazine. She was already home from work and had changed into a lime green muumuu with black flowers around the collar. Had she gone to a sale recently?

"You don't have to do this," she said.

"I want to do it." He put some body language into the phrase to show his determination, but it didn't work. "I haven't visited him in months."

"I'm not talking about visiting. I'm talking about what you plan to tell him."

"You mean those things I've been lying about my whole life? The things you suggested I talk to him about?"

"I wasn't serious, Clay. I was trying to make a point, and you took it literally."

Clay stalled, knowing he couldn't blame her. "It's best if I'm honest with him."

"Look," Lily said. "I applaud your decision to be honest, but ask yourself, does he really need to know? You're not being fair to your father. Think about his feelings."

Clay sighed. "I finally got my act together and am trying to be a better person, and now you're saying I should lie to him? I'm tired of lying."

"It's okay to lie sometimes," Lily said. "If someone's threatening you with violence because you're gay, it's okay to lie. If someone won't hire you because they think you're gay, it's okay to lie. If you think someone you love is going to be harmed because you're gay, it's okay to spare their feelings. You can lie. Don't do this to your dad. He's not as strong as you think."

"If I don't tell him," Clay said, "he'll just keep hounding me about getting married and having kids and keeping up the family name. I've made up my mind, Lily. I'm going to tell him, and I'm going to do it this weekend."

Then walking out the door, Clay muttered a quick affirmation under his breath. "You're smart and you can handle this. And if word gets around and the citizenry comes with torches and pitchforks, give me the strength to outrun them."

❖

It took him a little more than two hours to reach the hamlet of Bluebonnet, Mississippi. He'd known at a very early age that he couldn't stay in the small backwater delta town, and the people there must have known it too—another young person they couldn't restrain from leaving for a place with more opportunity.

The city's elders had tried to warn him about the cesspool that was New Orleans, providing sordid anecdotes as examples, but their stories only enticed him more. "I don't know why they have to sugarcoat everything," he joked to his friends who were also thinking of fleeing the small town.

Even though he had regular conversations with his father, Clay couldn't remember the last time he'd been home. It looked pretty much the same when he pulled into the driveway, though smaller, as if it had lost some of its power.

"Pop, I'm here." He opened the door to the home where he grew up, though it was never a place where he felt wanted or loved. It was a place of constant angst and unease—the source of never-ending dread for not living up to the expectations of parents who placed emphasis on status, achievement and morality.

Clay called out again and got the same silent response. Good. Time alone for a while. He walked up the stairs and down the hall to the bedroom where he'd spent thousands of hours, awake and asleep, doing homework, reading novels, hiding, scheming for the future, planning an escape. His heart was thumping.

The door stuck when he tried to open it, then creaked when it eventually swung inward. He was assailed with the scents of various cleaning products—furniture polish, air freshener—as well as clean linen and something that was unidentifiable, something musty but not offensive. The room was old, mellow and welcoming.

Everything seemed the same as it had been the last time. The walls were the same soft olive green that his mother had selected when he was in high school, just less vibrant now. The old quilt that covered the twin bed lay faded, even thinner and flatter. The baseball trophies were lined up on the bookshelf and the Bible study certificates framed in gilt frames.

It hadn't been easy, growing up as the son of a judge in this town, and Clay had felt the suffocating pressure. He knew that now. When he looked back, he could see that he'd been forced to fit into a mold, and was not allowed to figure out who he was. Maybe that was why he kept getting involved in weird alternative therapies.

He got no help from his father. Why couldn't he figure out that Clay was gay? He was a well-educated member of the bench, for crying out loud. Oh well, book smart, people stupid.

Clay dropped his bag and leaned down to click the switch on the box fan on the floor. Its whir was a comfort though he already felt shut in, claustrophobic at the thought of spending two nights in what he had once considered his prison but was now just a little room of memories.

When he heard the front door open, he walked to the top of the steps.

"There you are," Clay said.

"I was out shopping for dinner," the older man said. "I brought ribs to barbecue. That's one of your favorites, right?"

"Yessir," Clay lied. Ribs weren't his favorite at all. They were his father's favorite. Good job, Dad. He'd been there five minutes, and he'd already told a lie.

Clay told himself that it was okay, only a small fib with no consequences.

Throughout the rest of the evening, father and son prepared the evening meal, made small talk about weather, neighbors and city officials his father had known and worked with through the years, and about how much the town had changed. They made plans to visit Clay's mother's grave the next morning before going to the courthouse for the opening of the time capsule.

"You told me on the phone there was something that'd been bothering you," Clay said, finally broaching the subject after they had eaten.

"Yes, there is something bothering me—haunting me I guess you could say. Ever since your mother died." His deep-set eyes glanced down at the wedding ring that still adorned his finger.

Clay leaned in. He'd never heard his father talk like this.

"Your mother and I, we always tried to lead exemplary lives—what we used to call being fine upstanding citizens. But it dawns on me after all these years that we were frauds."

At first, Clay thought his dad might be joking, pulling his leg before he went onto the real topic. His father liked little jokes like that.

"What I am about to tell you in no way diminishes who you are or how much we love you."

"What is it?" Clay sat straight up in his chair.

"You were born out of wedlock," his father said solemnly.

"What?"

"The night before I shoved off for Korea, your mother and I, well—you get the idea. I was only supposed to do one tour of duty, but it ended up being longer. When I came home, there you were. Your mother, she'd gone off to her aunt's house in Cocodrie where no one knew who she was. She wore a ring she'd bought at Sears."

Clay's mind became fuzzy, a cloud of confusion.

"So," Clay finally babbled, "I'm a bastard?" He couldn't believe his ears. The walls had become squishy and seemed to move. All of a sudden, there was more drama in this kitchen than in any gay bar.

"No, of course not," his father said quickly. "Your mom's family knew the justice of the peace. He fudged everything. You're legitimate in the eyes of the law."

"Legitimate," Clay whispered. How lucky for me. He was on the verge of tears, but then it dawned on him that his parents had harbored more lies than he had and that gave him a perverted consolation.

"Just one thing," his father said. "The date on your birth certificate is not exactly accurate. You're one year older than the date it states. Sorry about that."

Clay's mind began to fog over and he got up to go to his bedroom. No Louise Hay affirmation was going to get him through this one.

❖

When he woke up the next morning, the first question he asked himself was how do I get out of here? He rubbed the sleep from his eyes and went to the bathroom. He cut a quick glance at himself in the mirror.

"You are a person of worth," he whispered. "You deserve all the good things that happen to you. And by the way, you're a bastard."

As he adjusted the shower nozzle, something dawned on him, so he returned to the mirror.

"And apparently, you are owed a gift for a missed birthday."

His father's deep voice called from downstairs. Clay could already smell bacon frying and the voice of the radio commentator Paul Harvey as he wound down one of his broadcasts with *The Rest of the Story*.

"Son, I'm making breakfast. It'll be ready in about five minutes."

So much for getting away from this place. Why had his father told him this information now? Clay didn't want to know. He could have lived the rest of his life without knowing the truth.

The longer he stood under the water, the angrier he grew with his father. If everyone was being honest these days, he'd toss out a few unpleasant truths of his own.

Clay seethed throughout breakfast and during the time they spent together at his mother's grave site. It was no shame to be born out of wedlock, and besides, no one knew. In fact, he could probably get quite a few laughs from his friends at the bar when he told this story. Better yet, he could write it down as a submission for the writers' group. Still, it bugged him—and he couldn't help wondering why his father had bothered to tell him, why he hadn't kept his secret.

"Forgive her," his father said from behind him. "Forgive both of us. We were young and stupid and didn't know what we were doing. Besides, you turned out all right."

His dad didn't know the half of it.

"You said you had something you wanted to talk about," his father said as they were driving to the courthouse.

"Mine can wait until we get through with the time capsule ceremony."

❖

Clay's dad stood at the podium in the overflowing hall of the courthouse. More than three hundred people had come out, a lot for a small town like Bluebonnet. The box had already been removed from a spot near the courthouse flagpole. The tin box had begun to decay and the city elders had already removed the lid. They'd found a commemorative letter from the mayor at the time, a bullet from World War I, a newspaper, a "Win-the-War" cookbook, a map of the state of Mississippi, two tickets to a screening of "Birth of a Nation" at the Tulane Theater in New Orleans, a baseball card featuring a Red Sox outfielder named Olaf Henriksen, and a Woodrow Wilson campaign button.

It had been decided by the planners to save the letter for last, when it would be read by a relative of the deceased. They wanted to end with a historical lesson, and perhaps a poignant moment from the Great War. Since the letter was penned by a member of the distinguished Byrd family, Clay's dad had been asked to read it.

"I never knew Uncle Tommy at all," Clay's dad had explained

on the way to the event. "He died before I was born. He was killed by a shell somewhere in France and no one ever discovered his remains. My family was devastated. I remember hearing his name many times while I was growing up. He supposedly was the life of the party, liked by everyone and he was also smart. It was a huge blow for the family and afterwards it was never quite the same, apparently."

But when it came time to open the letter, Clay's dad suddenly declined. "If it's okay with all of you, I think my son Clay should read the letter. Besides me, he's the last of the Byrd clan so far."

Clay's heart sank through the floor. He reluctantly trudged to the front of the room. The letter was handed to him and he opened it with great care. He coaxed the thin sheet of vellum out of an envelope adorned with a French stamp in red that featured a classically styled woman sowing seeds on a red background. He unfurled the letter and began to read.

My Dear Jack,

For the past summer I have tried to muster enough courage to write and tell you that everything between you and I must end.

What we have done, what we have felt for each other, will not work out in the heartless world we live in. Our love will never be accepted. I know in my heart that I love you, but it's not enough. My intentions are to get through this hellish war and return home, get married and raise a family. I recommend the same course of action for you.

Please know that you are with me forever. I think of you every day. Please forgive me and let us continue to be friends, no matter what happens.

With deepest love,
Tommy

When Clay finished and looked up, there was nothing but silence. No one moved.

"Would you like me to read it again?" he asked, a little spark of joy forming in his voice.

"I think we got the gist," said an alderman. He'd seen the stricken look on Judge Byrd's face and politely ushered Clay away from the podium. The event came to a quick close and attendees were instructed to *please* enjoy the fruit punch and cookies in the back of the room, and to visit the table that contained all the items in the time capsule.

Except for one.

❖

"That was interesting," Clay said when they were outside. He was starting to feel the glow of a goofy mood. "I wonder who Jack was."

"I don't have a clue," the old judge huffed. "Furthermore, I've never been so embarrassed in all of my life."

"I guess Tommy had a secret," Clay said. All of a sudden, the trip to Bluebonnet had been worth it. Turns out you could go home again; you just shouldn't stay too long.

"They would never have allowed that letter into the time capsule if they knew what it contained."

"No, they most certainly would not have," Clay said, and he began to laugh and couldn't stop. "The people of this community definitely wouldn't have let *that* slip by."

His laughter became uncontrollable, and he rocked back and forth in the passenger seat of the car, with only the seat belts restraining his motion. He'd still almost hit his head on the dashboard. Tears slid down his cheeks.

"What's the matter with you?" his father hissed, grabbing Clay's elbow. "Our family was just ridiculed in front of the whole town."

"Sorry," Clay said. But his entire body continued to shudder.

His father grew sullen. He took out his car keys.

"What happened to the letter?" Clay asked.

"It's right here."

"May I have it?"

"Whatever on earth would you want it for?"

"I might want to have it framed. To hang on the wall."

"Are you insane?"

"Not exactly," Clay said, though he realized that he had become giddy from all the laughter. There was a moment, when they were leaving the courthouse, when he decided it wasn't necessary now to tell his father about his own life and about the virus he carried. He might not be able to handle it, as Lily suggested. In his pride, he might disown his only son. Or he might die on the spot. Whatever the reason, Clay thought, it wasn't important now to burden his father with the truth.

"It's a sad story," Clay said.

"Why?" his father asked. A sour look had frozen on his face.

"Because he decided he'd live life as a lie, and then he got killed. I suspect he went to his death a very unhappy man." He felt a sense of kinship with this long-lost great-great-uncle who'd seen many of his friends wiped out before their prime, just as Clay had.

Later that night, after another round of barbecue ribs, Judge Armand Louis Byrd dropped the letter into Clay's lap. "Are you sure you want to take this with you?" he asked.

Clay had one of his goofy epiphanies, and he repurposed one of his affirmations.

"Dad," he said in a serious tone. "I *am* positive." With that, he made his statement of independence and related his sexual orientation and health status, even though it passed over the head of his father by a mile.

When he got home, he was surprised that Lily was out. Good, he thought, she'd finally gotten her ass off that couch and was out doing something.

He'd go to bed without telling her about his victory. He gazed into his eyes in the bathroom mirror, certain he was seeing someone new.

"You are a person of worth, Clayton Robert Byrd. You are smart and talented, and you have so much to offer. You have many obstacles, but you will find a way to deal with them. You will succeed at life because you are one lucky bastard."

PINEAPPLES

Patrick Earl Ryan

Okay, I'm guilty. I won't admit it to many people. But to Annie, I apologize. I completely forgot that it's her day. I'm awful at remembering things. I forget dentist appointments, birthdays, and the right exit for the DMV. These things wind up costing money. Late fees. Extra gas. Sometimes, when I go to bed, I think I have a tumor in my brain, just over my right eye, an inch and a quarter under my skull. I imagine a squadron of white blood cells blasting the giant gray blimp into a thousand fatty chunks. I fall asleep remembering they used to be me. This is the source of my forgetfulness. I daydream. I'm a grown man.

"Go with me to my nephew's big day," Annie suggests over the phone. I missed brunch at the Hummingbird. "You can still get here. He's in quiz bowl. It's your old high school. It'll be *so* fun. Half a day is better than nothing."

I know that without Annie days, I wouldn't do anything but teach driver's ed, read old copies of *Omni*, and make macaroni and cheese with six-for-a-dollar zucchini from Winn Dixie. She's always right, but in this case, it's not a bad thing. She has a way of focusing me on good things.

"Lucas needs our support," she says. "His dad is in Philadelphia this week. He likes you so much." I'm sure Lucas doesn't know me from the copy guy. But I was in quiz bowl in the seventh grade. My mom thought it would be healthy if I competed in team sports. When I tried out for track and field, I twisted my ankle when I stumbled into the pole vault pit. Running was the only thing I thought I could do, but I was slower than spit from a cow, according to our coach. My annoying habit of giving away the answers to Jeopardy questions before my mom could guess them convinced her I'd be perfect for quiz bowl. No one else on the team enjoyed me being there, either. I freaked out in front of the audience at the city's semi-finals. I forgot the capital of Mozambique. I forgot the riddle of the Sphinx. I spilled my glass of water on Tim Brewster's lap, and it was *all* caught on video.

I almost tell Annie that I can't go with her today. "Come on," she says. "You know you want to go. You and Lucas get along. You'd give him encouragement. Weren't you in quiz bowl, anyway?"

❖

The school put in the west wing the year after I graduated. When I was in quiz bowl, we squeezed eight tables onto the basketball court and divided them with gym rope and orange safety cones. I could've benefited from PCs and overhead projectors. Annie has other things on her mind. She walks down the wide carpeted hall without minding anyone in her path. "In a mood today, aren't you?" We pass the cupcakes and punch in the hallway. Her hair is shorter than last weekend. She must've seen Tazio. Pampering herself, but mad at the world—she's obviously been dumped.

"I'm breaking up with Tazio," she admits as soon as we pick our seats. "I've had enough of his love/hate dilemma. It's freaky when you can watch a person behave exactly like his psychological profile says he'll behave...*and* my sister said he came on to her at our Christmas party!"

"Who? Margie?"

"No, not Margie. Tara. The lesbian."

"Oh so he's a doofus, too?"

"You always make me feel better."

The cameraman, who looks a lot like my dad, nudges past us. I tell Annie, "You know, I never liked Tazio anyway. He's so hairy."

"Oh, it doesn't matter. It's done. It's unforgivable. He should've known better. You don't have to worry about me. I found another ball of yarn already. He's from Bolivia. He's a policeman."

"I thought you didn't date men from South America," I say. "Or for that matter, policemen either."

"Oh, be quiet," she says. "The questions are starting."

His stubby eyebrows descend on close-set but bright eyes, the early dip of a cleft chin, Baryshnikov as a teenager. Something of that 70s Soviet chic, too, in his shaggy hair an inch longer than his friends'. His lips pout, shoulders hunch. He sniffs and clears his throat. He ignores the nervous, meaningless chatter of his teammates and scribbles away on a yellow sheet of paper.

When the competition starts, he answers six questions correctly in a row, buzzing with a quick slap of his palm as if the button were a fly. Annie whispers to me, "Wow, he's smarter than you."

"Goldfish," he answers again, and I learn, among other things, the strings of a violin are tuned at intervals of fifths, geotropism is the tendency for plants to grow toward light, a fathom measures six feet, the king of Russia at the turn of the eighteenth century was Peter the Great, and the equation for momentum is far too hard for me to remember, until finally, it's over. Everyone claps for the winners, a few for the losers, but I clap for Lucas. Each of the boys shakes hands with his fellow competitors. After oohs and aahs, they pose for a bifocaled photographer.

From the crowd, Hannah, Lucas' sister, slinks through with her golden smile to embrace Annie. They could be sisters. "How am I doing with the driving?" Hannah asks me, still hugging Annie.

"You could work on that shaky braking," I say. She's in her third day of classes in driver's ed. I'm her instructor. I always get the Catholic school kids. "But not too bad. Nothing practice won't iron out."

"I'll be perfect by prom night, right?"

"Oh, the prom!" Annie squeaks. "That's so cute! You're gonna drive your date?"

"Yeah," Hannah says. "But only cause Raven doesn't have a car yet. Otherwise he'd be driving."

"Oh, I have a brilliant idea," Annie nearly yells into my ear. "You can give Hannah extra lessons…just, you know…on the side. I used to be *aw*ful at braking. Ask Evan, absolutely scary!"

But I only half hear her request. I agree to help Hannah, but I don't remember the stipulations. Instead, I remember the peculiar way Lucas wrinkles his forehead, arching his eyebrows, whenever he's charged with a compliment, as if some nerve twinges beneath the surface in embarrassment. It isn't until we're out the building and we're walking back to my car that Annie stops me, percolating devilishness, and says, "You have a crush on my nephew, don't you?"

❖

It isn't an hour I expect to enjoy or even spend without distress. I know Hannah's driving skills. She doesn't know the location or the use for a parking brake. Frustrated, she looks back and forth between speedometer and back window, attempting to pull out of the driveway still in neutral. Impatient, she doesn't adjust her mirrors or her over-reclined seat. Drifting blithely backward down the slight slope of their driveway, she squashes several of her mom's daisies and nearly topples their canary yellow mailbox. To each folly, she reacts with a "Fuck!," as if she's never allowed to curse at home; but in the driver's seat, with that swelling kernel of adult responsibility, caught up in her anxiety over failing and killing her driving instructor in the process, she says "Fuck!" abundantly, amending each curse with the same horror at her own tongue, "Oh my God, I'm so sorry, Mr. Evan!" Then she checks the rearview mirror every few seconds, faithfully, and leading me to wonder if lessons really do sink in, but then she runs a single finger across her lower lip, blots the edges of her mouth with the same finger as if she's checking for the remnants of a long-gone cold sore, and asks me, "Do I have lipstick on my teeth?"

I can see a bit of Lucas' features in the snowy gleam of her forehead, in the pink, almost drunken flush in her cheeks. "You're doing so well. But try to keep both your hands on the steering wheel."

"Oh, right."

"Now, right here, be a little gentler with the brake. Don't stomp on it like a cockroach."

I know Lucas would learn one hundred percent quicker than his sister. He'd slouch like a juvenile delinquent playing hooky, controlling the car as easily as one of his video games. While I'm lost in a thought and Hannah is lost in the annoying bend of an eyelash, we coast straight through a red light at Robert E. Lee and into a bus stop pole. I feel guilty, as Hannah sighs again, "Fuck."

❖

I can't concentrate when I'm in love, and this morning, I woke to love. Even though every one of my crushes has turned out badly, I've decided that just the act of falling in love is beneficial on its own, regardless of any outcomes. It's good for the heart and a sense of compassion. I decide these things on my way to work, motivated by an energy drink in a skinny orange can and my original cast recording of *Rent*. My students would say I teach better in this charmed condition—if they knew the reasons behind the charm. I give them longer breaks. I don't mark them off for missing exits or merge signs. I tell more stories, like today's on my grandfather's predilection for running people off the highway when they failed to signal properly.

On lunch break I hide in the little yellow break room, pretending to grade tests, chewing the erasers off pencils, planning a whole new life off this young love. I call Annie because she's always home on Tuesdays. One phone line comes back to the break room. The other three are for business only. The first thing she says to me is: "You know, we *all* think Lucas is gay. We've been thinking it for years."

"Who are *we*, Annie?"

"Us. The family. Everyone," she says.

I open my bag of chips. It's strange, I've bought the same chips since I was a kid. They don't even use the same recipe. Everything has a new flavor. Nothing can just be corn and oil and Annie cannot tell a truthful story. She accentuates. It's important to take this into consideration.

"He got his Internet privileges taken away last year because Margie found a bunch of emails with *really* nasty conversations in them. Like porn quality. And you know how my family behaves about sex. Him and his little friend were chatting with some old guy in Nebraska like every freaking night, talking about getting naked together, sucking big dicks, *all* of your favorite things."

"Lucas? Lucas did that?" I ask in thorough doubt. "Geez…I didn't even know he had his own email."

Frieda, the last of the classroom teachers, moseys into the break room and slides a diet frozen dinner into the employee microwave. The other teachers have all quit—not in protest or disgust, just strange coincidences. Frieda always wears primary red lipstick and powders her face ethereal white. While the microwave heats her chicken piccata, she switches on the RCA television that our boss only recently mounted over the table and finds *The Young and the Restless*. "Oh, Lord," she starts in. "Holden's gonna be gettin' into trouble again. Look at that girl. Barely got panties on. He's always cozying up to them like that. But he's all additives and preservatives!"

"Can you turn down the volume though…just for a minute?" I interject. I eat another chip, stare, and wait. She notices the phone, but I make it obvious and shake it like a maraca.

"Oh, I'm sorry, hun," she says.

"You should be his role model," Annie continues. "He *really* likes you."

"You think?"

"He never smiles at anyone. His mom calls him 'stone face.' Didn't he smile at you at quiz bowl?"

"I guess."

Frieda watches the quieter television with hammed up enthusiasm, pinching prudently at the corners of her hot lunch, trying to remove the plastic wrap without looking down. "Oh, anyway, listen," Annie says. "I have a date with this doctor tonight. He's twenty…mmm, no, maybe twenty-five pounds overweight, but his ears are *so* adorable. They stick straight out. Doesn't that mean something in China? And he knows how to give head *so* good. I need help. Should I get stoned first?"

That afternoon, Lucas' parents are leaving the house as I turn onto their street. They spot the Harold Moss driving school car because of the large red letters across the side and wave to me as if I were the ice cream man. I have no excuse for being here. I tell them, "I had some extra time. If Hannah's around, I thought I'd offer some more practice time before her exams? Is she around?"

"Nope," Fred says. "It's just Lucas and the Dark Lord upstairs."

"Oh, damn. I guess another time then."

"How are you, honey?" Margie asks. "Go on up and see Lucas instead. He said you like video games. Don't get hooked. I wound up sneaking into his room when he was at school to play SimCity!"

"Oh, Lucas…okay, I…"

"Okay, see ya, buddy," Fred says. "We've got salsa class. Come by on Sunday for barbeque!"

I don't go right up. Fred and Margie bought this house two years ago, and from top to bottom, everything is new. When you come from a mom who thinks cigarette smoke adds character to the furniture, a spotless, state-of-the-art kitchen is a beautiful thing. I examine the photos posted across the refrigerator with butterfly magnets. I wait, eat a grape, read their grocery list.

Lucas, by now, must think he's home alone. I would.

When I was thirteen, I knew a heck of a lot for my age. I knew how to drive a car well enough to make it to Popeye's and not get pulled over by any cops. I knew how to make pancakes from scratch. I knew how to jack off anywhere, on public buses, in stairwells, in convenience stores, and ached for every possible chance to yank it, without exhaustion or boredom. This is the evidence I cite when I approach Lucas' room, imagining the best of my dreams, but he just sits dully in the middle of his bedroom floor, battling monsters and demons with the fanciest and largest joystick I've ever seen and a gigantic bowl of assorted-flavor jelly beans nudged crookedly between his crossed legs. Today, he's wearing khaki shorts. Summer is a good time. This is the center. This is the atom. That space where everything coalesces.

"Hey, you," he says. I'm just peeking into the door. He doesn't seem surprised to see me there.

"Your mom let me up," I explain.

"Oh," he says. "You're not taking Hannah out for a lesson?"

"Nope."

Video game magazines and cartridges, some opened, some taken apart, some torn into two, some still in sealed boxes, cover his entire bedroom floor in a crowded order. "Your mom said Hannah is out for the night."

"Lucky her."

I open my mouth and find it heavy and hushed with a clever response that just won't coalesce. "Oh," I say. "Everybody gets lucky."

Embarrassed by my own rubbish, I read the game titles. The collection spans the alphabet. *BioShock 2: Minerva's Den*, *Halo: Combat Evolved*, *Resident Evil 4*, *World of Warcraft: Wrath of the Lich King*.

"Most of those aren't mine," he says once I've come full circle. "My friends leave them here."

I push a few of the games under his bed so I can sit on the floor beside him. His fingers move as fast as fleas over the joystick. His socked foot nudges my pinkie finger. The bottoms of his socks are grubby with dust and pet hair. The sock on his other foot has a hole from his big toe to his fourth toe—beyond purpose. He keeps his eyes on the flickering screen but doesn't move his foot away from my hand for a full eighteen seconds. I count through it to myself.

"Do you wanna try playing?"

"You know," I answer, truthfully frowning. "I don't think I'd get very far."

"Okay, your loss," he teases.

❖

"The fucking doctor chickened out on me," Annie complains over the phone. "He says his parents are in town. He's fifty-four! His fucking loss. Who wouldn't love a night with these titties? I mean, come on! Ugh, I need you. Please, I'll pay for everything. I'll bring a joint for afterward. I'll keep my mouth shut about men…I promise. Just have dinner with me at Carmen's. You love Carmen's. We can get a pitcher of sangrias. They have those spicy calamari."

I hear that old desperation like high school—desperate to be with someone, desperate to talk about her feelings. I'm good at listening. I have a soft spot for her like this. The guilt-free dinners with her when she's been jilted by a lover are some of the best I've had; it's hard to get reservations at Carmen's, a hip Cuban restaurant with seven tables and three cheap, colorful paintings.

I show up wearing the same baggy jeans and Billabong t-shirt I wore to Lucas' house. The rain's poured since sunset and I'm a few drops from drenched. I feel seven years old. She's out of Prozac, dressed in a dry flowy white blouse and a tight skirt cut above the knees in the same purple as the dahlia tucked behind her ear. She walked in that practically graceful way she acquires when she's had a big toke before leaving her house. This is her Frida Kahlo look. Her words. She'll sulk and smoke French cigarettes again. She'll sneer and cut in front of men in long lines.

We order the fried spicy calamari, holding onto our water glasses, watching the empty chairs wobble as a big truck passes on the street. She tells me, "I think I want to date women again."

Deluded with one, she runs for the other.

"Anyone specific in mind?" I ask her.

"Of course not…Mmm, well there is this one research fellow… but I don't mix work and sex. You have to help me. Set me up."

"Annie, 'women' disqualifies ninety-five percent of the people I know. How could *I* possibly help *you*?"

"Ugh…you need more lesbian friends." When we're waiting for our chicken and sausage paella, she leans closer to me, and I think we're about to make fun of the man eating his *ensalada boniato* with his fingers at the next table, but she turns serious and tells me, "So, listen…be careful with Lucas. Try to be a good role model. Fred is really weird about the gay thing."

"Really? Your sister's not."

"Yeah, Margie doesn't care about anything. She's like me."

"I think Lucas likes me," I tell her, though I'm not sure I believe that. "I just get that hunch."

"Really? Oh, that's so cute," she cheeps, an instant gap in her hard-shelled crust because Annie is always helpless in the presence of love, and any love, without prejudice, wishing the world to be inundated with love. "You both have a crush. I haven't seen you blush since Whitey!"

"So what should I do?"

Maybe she knows the answer, but she doesn't share it. She spreads butter on her warm baguette then ponders the knife. But the lights go out. The restaurant is damned into twilight vagueness. It's the heavy rain. Annie giggles, "I wonder if it's someone's birthday!" Another passing truck rattles the forks on our table. Its headlights illuminate us all again. Annie licks butter from her fingers. The man beside us sips carefully from his hefty margarita. Our waitress stands mystified at the kitchen counter. Then it's the dark again—and it feels secret, like communion.

Someone from the back calls out, "It will all be fine in a few moments. Just pretend you're at the shows!" The rain edges louder. A person behind us chews ice. "Lucas seems pretty brilliant," I continue our conversation. "For any age, really. I mean…he's just like me at that age."

"Well, you were never in honors."

"No. I mean it. I'm seriously not into kids. He just seems so… special. He needs inspiration."

"Just be careful," she says. "Fred would totally freak out. He had some bad childhood experiences…Oh my God, do you smell that? That smells so incredible. This will make me forget everything!"

The waitress finds her way to our table with our steaming calamari. "Ugh…you two lovebirds…"

❖

Reluctantly, I pick up Hannah on Sunday morning for her second free lesson. This time, she's waiting in the driveway, bubble gum in her mouth, neon scrunchies in her bleached hair. "Thanks for the lessons," she mumbles when she gets into the driver's seat. "Mom says I should give you twenty dollars," so she hands me a folded damp bill. "Sorry, I just got home from cheerleading practice."

She's worked on her braking, though not an awful lot. She approaches the first stop sign as hesitant as an ant. "Oh, I brought a tape," she squeaks, pulling a cassette from the sundry contents of her tiny pink purse. "My boyfriend made me a mixtape. He makes them all the time. It probably sucks."

She talks endlessly about nothing. Primps in the rearview mirror at every stoplight. The mixtape definitely sucks. "Pretty soon, Lucas will need lessons, too," I offer as small talk that I might be interested in, then turn the volume lower on grating guitars and a lead singer who sounds as if he needs to blow his nose. "Will you and him both be driving your dad's old minivan?"

"Dad won't let him drive for another two years."

"Oh, but he could get a learner's permit."

"I know," she sighs. "Ain't that the shits?"

Lucas is stringing pineapple party lights across the front yard when we pull into the driveway. The late morning sun glimmers in the plastic bulbs and at the proper angle through his golden hair. The cruel sister—Hannah honks the horn six times even though I tell her, "Please don't do that" after the second honk and Lucas plugs his ears with his fingers and yells, "Goofball!"

"Thanks again for the lesson. Tell my Aunt Annie to come see us," Hannah says, grabbing her purse out of the back seat and rushing into the house. "Mom! Did Raven call? Mom! Ughhhhhhh, where *are* you?!"

I scoot into the driver's seat just as Lucas comes to my window. "Did she run over any old ladies?" he asks, then calls out after Hannah's gone inside and closed the door, "Mom's not home!"

"She's getting the hang of it," I say. I sound like my fifth-grade math teacher. I failed geometry twice.

"She's such a dweeb," he complains. "It's nice of you to give her lessons, but she's a dweeb."

"Yeah...I, uh..."

He leans against the door. Scratches a pebble from the bottom of his sneakers. He has fashion sense. Everything he wears looks brand new. I didn't have fashion sense at his age. I wore stripes with prints. Hand-me-down jackets that were two sizes too big. T-shirts from Chess King.

"I like your glasses," he tells me.

"Oh, thanks...I guess I haven't worn these out of the house before. Where's your mom? Everyone's out?"

"They're at mass," he says. "I don't want to go to church anymore so she's making me decorate the front lawn. We're having another pool party. Fifty of Hannah's friends and two of mine."

"Oh, right," I say, admiring what looked like festive, finished decorations. "Are you all finished?"

"Yeah, you like it?"

"I do. Expert job."

And he beams.

"Well, you know, I was thinking of driving out to the movies with Annie now. You want to tag along since you're all done with your chores? I'd get you back in time. It's that new Schwarzenegger flick."

"Schwarzenegger?" he asks. "Really?"

It's a thin, porous fabrication. Annie is at yoga class on Sunday nights. I have a psychological aversion to bodybuilders and their balloon muscles. But a shoot 'em up blockbuster seems like a good bet for a kid who likes shoot 'em up video games. "I wanted to see that," he admits, and my heart, my cock, and the thick vein down the right side of my neck thump in strong, quick rhythm, my fingers drum the steering wheel, and I'm about to choke on my own spit.

He smells like grass, acorns, and the yellow dust that coats everything. His old sweat saturates every molecule of air in my car. It's as if a seed has burst—the clarity and deep impression inside me.

He wiggles his legs against the seat and whistles. The sky dances, too. Clouds like falling blankets.

Lucas doesn't ask me why we don't pick up his Aunt Annie. Maybe he thinks she'll be meeting us there. The Empire is the newest cineplex in New Orleans, halfway into the boondocks. The planners couldn't fit the 20-screen movie palace anywhere else. When I was a kid, this was a mall with a huge arcade and roller-skating rink, but they leveled everything after the last hurricane. The new building is supposed to look like a Roman temple, but in these swampy woods, it's more like a plantation. Rotting bougainvilleas creep up the plaster white columns.

As the first drops of an afternoon thunderstorm splat over mini-vans and pickup trucks, Lucas and I dash for the awning. No one around has an umbrella. Everyone wants to cool off. There's that blockbuster feeling of anticipation.

People must think I'm his dad or big brother. From the pit of my stomach, a deep grumble rises in my chest to my throat like a nausea of cluttered thoughts. My steps are so graceless. The whole world seems to watch. When I refuse to let him pay for his ticket, he tells me, "You don't really need to do that. I know I'm young and all. But I actually make lots of money. More than Hannah with her pink bows. I still get an allowance, too. I'm saving for medical school…and maybe a dot-com." He pushes his crisp, smoothed twenty under the glass with the assurance of a millionaire.

"You did great in quiz bowl," I tell him after the doorman returns our stubs. "I was in quiz bowl, too."

"Oh yeah?"

"*So* many years ago."

"Was Mister Carl your advisor?"

"Um…no. Was that the guy with the orange tie?" I wonder if he knows any of these other boys whooshing past us with their skinny arms around giant sodas and overflowing popcorns, but he doesn't say hello to anyone. "Brother Barry ran everything," I remember just as I decide to say his name. "Like a Nazi."

"That's so funny! He's the disciplinarian now. My friend Dudley got his ass whipped in Brother Barry's office. I mean, like, his actual ass. I heard he keeps a two-foot wooden switch in his desk."

In the theater, the dark red seats smell like brand new cars, butter, and old soda. Maybe a dozen other people are in the theater with us. Lucas, fingers already dipping into the popcorn, beats me to answering every trivia question that comes across the screen. I lie to him, "I watch foreign movies."

"So are you gonna give me free driving lessons, too, teach?" he asks just when the lights dim and the older, rowdier teens hoot along to the first chords of Twentieth Century Fox's fanfare.

"Sure," I answer, "As many as you want," but the music bursts out like raging floodwater from a broken levee, and he doesn't hear anything I said. In the kaleidoscope dark, I can still distinguish him from the nothing around him. His small straight nose rimmed by the yellow aisle light.

The movie lends itself to losing myself in my thoughts. It's one of those apocalyptic, evil reincarnated, renegade hero blockbusters. I scoop a handful of popcorn into my hand, eat it, and unintentionally touch Lucas' knee—the rough, new denim. Aliens wipe out half the world in the first thirty minutes. I make little hearts on his jeans with my finger. I don't know what he's thinking. He cringes and then giggles at the same tacky dialogue as I do. His eyes widen as a jade sword pierces Satan's heart. But when the credits roll and the lights go up, he only says, "Fun!"

"Yeah...fun!"

This is the beginning of a new life, I decide. We'll do *fun* things together. We can sneak behind people's backs. I can teach him wise things about the world that can't be learned from books. When we're speeding down the I-10 at eighty miles per hour, I say to him, "I like you, Lucas."

"I know," he says. "Thanks for taking me to the movies."

"You know?" I ask him. I hear a helicopter pass over us. The rain stopped while we watched the movie and now a bright afternoon sky spreads around us and the day's worth of puddles and wet pavement evaporates so quickly we watch it happen. The white-tipped weeds have already grown taller. A simmering haze rises from the ground. "I mean I *like* you...Jesus...I probably sound like an idiot."

I pass the exit to his house. It isn't a thought or a plan. I just want this to continue. I pass another exit and he says, "You missed Bonn..." but I assure him, "I know, I know. It's fine," even though saying it leaves a green haze of self-doubt. My foot remains on this gas pedal. My hands grip this steering wheel without turns. "I just kinda got the feeling…that maybe you liked me, too…" Together, we soar to somewhere that isn't New Orleans. A cabin in the Mississippi woods. A motel room with dark curtains and snack machines. Even I can hear the wrong in my thoughts. But the sun inspires a promise—however blind or false. We pass the WELCOME TO SAINT TAMMANY PARISH sign. Narrow asphalt shoulders give way to thick woods where the trees grow taller.

"Can you bring me home now?" Lucas asks. I hadn't thought to look away from the panoramic view. His bottom lip and childish chin quiver. Sweat glistens his forehead. His small, pink hands squeeze together, and a tear rolls to the corner of his lip. "I want to go home. Can you bring me home, please?"

Dark oaks bow low—inches above the many cars squeezed into every parking space along Lucas' street. Foregoing an invitation to the pool party, I only pull in front of the driveway, set the brake, and turn off the car. The engine still creaks and sets. The fuzzy yellow glow from Lucas' crisscrossed party lights leaves everything else in murky blues. Nothing I can say will change things, not that I even know which words would, and words push out at my chest and swell up in my mouth. His youth frightens me. His youth leaves him emotional and unreasonable. His youth can be wielded—protects him. "I didn't mean to scare you," I blurt. "I just thought…I wasn't planning to…"

But he leaves.

Halfway across the yard he turns back to me, frowns, and waves, a folding of fingers, without lifting his arm, without drying his wet-cheeked, red-eyed face. His deepness and sincerity baffle me. His emotions seem so swollen and tender. I feel guilty for judging—but his distress feels so enormous for the smallness of our afternoon. I wave and try to grin, but it probably looks like a wince. He's already inside his house by the time Annie sashays to the car window with a cat's grin.

"Babe! Come have a sangria!"

"Oh, no, no. I shouldn't stay parked…"

"Just come grab a to-go cup!"

"I…mmm, it wouldn't…"

What might seem like uncertainty on my face offers her an invitation to ensnare me: "You totally flaked on me today. You always flake on me! Come on, you owe me! I have your favorite!"

By the time I'm lured to the sidewalk by guilt and the sleek, tight joint she tucked between her tits, she's already pranced back to the fence to drag her salt-and-pepper-haired doctor away from his chatty crowd. "No, no, no. You have to come meet him now," I hear her implore in her sing-songy tipsy voice. I wish to myself that Lucas doesn't see me. "If he likes you, then we're golden!"

But it's Fred I hear above everyone else, "Hey!" as a long grunt, "Hey, pervert!" A hush mushrooms around him as he stomps toward me. It doesn't seem like a joke. "Hey! Don't walk away from me!" he yells—I don't think I'm moving. "What did you do!" his voice cracks. "What did you do to my son to make him cry?" He can float away with all of that anger in his chest. He's already answered his question, no matter my friendship with Annie, persuaded by some unshakeable emotion. All of me—inside and out—shrinks away from him and the attention he's drawn. I feel his accusations branded into my forehead. Someone says, "Come on, guys, kids are here…"

I should run.

But Margie comes out, too. She reaches out her little hand to him. I even hold my breath. He jerks his shoulder away. "You said you wouldn't," she tries repeatedly, pleads with the back of his head, his red face, and his tight jaw. She steps between us. "Just go," she orders me. "You need to get away from here, Evan…I'm sorry. Please. Just go… really. Go, really. It won't get better."

Mouth agape, Annie strides up, the frilly ends of her long black skirt catching on the hedges, and is met with a shaky roar, "Stay out of this, Annie. It's none of your business!" Then he points at me. "You don't get to mess around with my son! I know what you fucking freaks do!"

"Hey, come on, this isn't the right time…"

"You don't get to touch my son!"

"Can someone go get Uncle Jim?"

"Fred, baby, what are you doing? You don't need to do this. This is Annie's friend. We know Evan."

"Fuck Annie's friends!"

"I don't…I…"

"Hey, come on now, hey…hey!"

The warm heft of his fist into my face surprises me. I can't even say whether he struck my nose, my cheek, my jaw. My face caves beneath thick bones. A swollen shock. The force explodes in my ears— like falling through the surface of water, like the Gulf's wild waves crashing into my head. I spin. My ankles twist. My heels slip out. The cool sidewalk. That memory of cool asphalt of a schoolyard. The cement vibrates with my bones. Then the hard toe of his shoe kicks me. Kicks me again. I even wonder how I could feel so little. It's Annie's voice I hear shouting, "Stop it, no, Fred! Stop it, you're hurting him!" Already my eyebrows feel swollen three times larger and I can only see blurs of grays and browns—save for the two pineapple lights shimmering above my head, multiplying into four, then eight…back again to those two yellow eyes. Those eyes—if only I can just lock on to them like a lover's gaze and never look away.

THE FOG HOUSE

Colby Byrne

I had a new message from a girl calling herself Heath. Short for Heathcliff, it turned out. She read a poem I posted on my blog when I was feeling self-indulgent and looking for the artistic validation my professors wouldn't give me. It was about myself, but also about Wuthering Heights, which I had just read in my Victorian Literature course and was subsequently obsessed with. Not that I especially enjoyed the experience of reading the novel itself, it's just that I knew getting caught up in its gothic cult following would make me feel interesting.

All over my little blog were images from different *Wuthering Heights* movies, countless quotes like Cathy's iconic, "He's more myself than I am," and clips from Kate Bush's music videos—and you can bet I was blasting that song on repeat. I loved showing off on my blog like that, looking more academic than I really was. Like I was the kind of person who could actually be touched by a work of literature— one from the 19th century, no less. Not many in my real life viewed me as an intellectual, or even as artistic. Just quiet. Here on my blog with a decent audience, I was cultured, esoteric even. I liked to think they pictured me like Kate Bush in that music video, with flowing see- through fabrics, gracefully throwing myself onto a grassy hill. "He's so…effervescent," they'd say.

Heath's message read:

"Beautiful poem.…We are happy to find another looking for Emily's truth…*/*…Do you know about >>Fog<< (1999)?"

I loved her immediately. It felt like a major accomplishment that a person with such an ethereal messaging style and casual familiarity with a Brontë sister appreciated my work. I went to her blog. It had a black background, and was programmed so the viewer's mouse looked like a single blinking eye when swept across the screen.

I scrolled through her posts: a series of phone pictures taken of a grainy video game on a fancy TV, burning candles always lit on either side. Beneath each photo, there was no description, just a date. A photo had been posted every day for as far back as I bothered to scroll. And I scrolled for a while.

The game on the screen always depicted the back of a male figure dressed in a black overcoat walking through a dense fog. Most of the shots were nearly indiscernible from one another, while some gave a better sense of the scenery this little man was traveling, filled with deep green hills, and occasional stone paths.

I opened a new tab and googled "Fog game 1999" and found a brief Wikipedia article about a Japanese video game very loosely based on Wuthering Heights, where you play as an exorcist in the moors, assisting various strangers haunted by ghosts. The game was never released outside of Japan.

I messaged Heath back, trying to sound as cool as she did without looking like a poser:

"Interesting…how did you find it? Your blog feels like a dream~~"

I felt self-conscious about the "~~" but decided not to think about it too much. Later that night I got a response:

"Julia did. There's a secret If your soul is open. ///We'd like to show you some day.///"

Heath and I had a back and forth for about a month. It turned out she was living with her girlfriend, Julia, in a farmhouse in upstate New York. Julia's family was wealthy, and this past year, they allowed her and Heath to move in there together. The two of them had recruited a few people over the course of the year to live as a unit in what they dubbed "The Fog House."

"Why did they come there?"

"To find Cathy."

Julia was collecting like-minded people who were willing to follow her on her search for Cathy. In that sense, she was like Heathcliff pining after his beloved Cathy's ghost in the novel. But this was also different.

"Cathy isn't ghost————,.+ Cathy is really God."

I'm sure most would have blocked her right then and there, but I decided to hear her out. I was a friendless college freshman at a big university then. My roommate was always out partying, and I spent most of my weekend nights reading blogs, drinking boxed wine until I threw up, taking Tums, and feeling sorry for myself. I've been on a range of antidepressants since middle school, when a severe case of social anxiety took over. I wouldn't talk to people unless directly approached, and even then, I would resent a person for forcing me to engage. I could always find a reason why anything I was saying was wrong or disturbing, so I was constantly deleting sentences in my head midway through speaking them. Conversations would always end with a string of jumbled words floating in the air, and my unsettled audiences excusing themselves politely.

Over time, my anxiety became less severe, but that didn't mean my social life suddenly blossomed. Any hopes of making new and interesting friends in college were dashed, and by the time the spring semester of my freshman year began, I had come to terms with the fact that I was, by nature, a person meant to be alone. Fine! I believed in me, and my entire value system was based around that self-preservation. I liked to think of myself as someone who thought nothing mattered, but this was difficult to reconcile with the fact that I also mattered a whole fucking lot.

In high school, I had gone through brief stints of satanic worship to counter my parent's vehement Christianity, but I never had the discipline to stick with it. I just liked the idea of being led by the dark. I guess that's what drew me to Wuthering Heights. So, did I think Julia and Heath were crazy for believing that God was hidden somewhere deep inside a bad video game? Who's to say? If God really was so elusive, why wouldn't Fog (1999) be the exact place to find him? Or her, rather. Loving Jesus stopped being edgy millenniums ago, so maybe these two figured out a nice alternative. I can't say their complimenting my poetry didn't sway me to give them the benefit of the doubt.

"The fog is endless. You run forever; when you stop running… God gives up on you."

"What happens when you find her?"

"You can see."

I told Heath my spring break was coming up, and she said Julia wanted to meet me. I bit the bullet and drove six hours to the Fog House, thinking about the Amish a lot as I went through Pennsylvania. It was less of a farmhouse and more of a mansion with a barn. There were acres of open land, woods, and a long gravel driveway. I pulled up next to the house and got out of my car.

Heath watched me from the porch then walked over to stand about a yard from me, her hands crossed in front of her, and bare feet digging into one another. She had enormous, curly hair in a middle part and dark circles under her eyes. She wore a billowing cotton black dress with a plaid red blanket draped across her shoulders.

"You're tall," she shouted, as if she were very far away. She had an indiscernible accent and a look in her eyes that also felt distant. "Julia will be happy." She never smiled.

I followed her in the side door of the house, and was immediately struck by a burning herbal smell and sounds of a piano playing in the distance. There was a large circular table with several chairs surrounding it, and a candelabra at its center. Heath took my bags from me and led me down a long, dim hallway. The walls were lined with watercolors on ripped sheets of paper, each portraying two eyes emerging from a gray mass that varied in size and intensity from painting to painting.

We came to an open room with a high ceiling and wooden beams, and there was Julia painting on an easel. She had straight dark hair tied in a ponytail and wore a white linen dress that looked expensive. In one hand was a crystal glass filled with bright pink liquid. When she noticed us, she stood up with a cheerful smile, put her glass down, and floated over on her bare feet. She embraced me, and whispered in my ear,

"Never turn your brights on in the fog." She pulled away to stare into my eyes, and I became paranoid that she saw something there. But then she laughed as if this whole thing were a joke, and downed the rest of her pink drink. "It's so nice to finally meet you!"

I had a really nice weekend that first visit. She showed me the house and the property, the horses, the very normal-seeming caretaker that she called Joseph—though I got the sense that wasn't his real name. There was also a girl who had recently graduated from a fancy woman's college at the house named Amy. She seemed normal and smart, like she had a sense of humor. And then there was Vlad, a nearly mute, muscular blonde guy.

The five of us had a picnic that first evening out in the field, even though it was still pretty chilly. Julia served expensive rosé in crystal glasses, then vodka mixed with pink lemonade and club soda. Fancy cheese and breads on the side. My teeth hurt from the sugar, but I remember laughing a lot during the picnic. Julia was full of one-liners, and would tell these crazy stories of voyages she'd been on in Europe, lovers she'd had, and the time she visited her brother with a coke problem in Thailand. Everything she talked about became funny and full of life, and I remember thinking to myself she could be a famous person. She had the look, the charm, the intellect, definitely the money. What was she doing here?

Eventually, as the sun was setting over the field, Heath began cleaning up glasses and plates, and asked for Amy and Vlad's help. I offered, but Julia told me to stay. She asked me about myself, about my family, friends, college. I told her I didn't really have friends and wasn't close to my parents, that they were extremely Christian conservatives and we didn't get along very well.

"Funny how you turned out the way you did in spite of that," she said with a validating smile. She was amazing at making you feel seen. "Why do you think that is?"

Julia was the first person I came out to in real life. I had told others online I was gay, but never a physical human. I'd been called "fag" plenty in school of course, but never confirmed or denied those accusations. Funny how I had just met her hours earlier, and there I was, tipsy and confessing the thing I blamed most for my weaknesses.

I didn't agonize over the issue of my gayness when I was younger; I just kind of accepted it because it would be so exhausting not to. It didn't give me the grief you'd think it would coming from such a religious home, but rather, it felt like a justification for any bad thought I might have had. It pushed me to believe things about myself that weren't true. The floodgates were open to all the evils out there by letting myself be gay. And it felt like, if I let anyone else in on that secret, they'd immediately see me for everything else I was and wasn't—some deranged, amoral deviant. "If he could be gay, he could also be a killer, a rapist, or even an atheist."

So, I guess it wasn't about being gay, even though being gay had everything to do with it. And yet, I wanted Julia to see me for who I was. I wanted her to see all that. And if she could, and could still like me, it didn't matter so much that I was evil. She hugged me when I told her, and I almost started to cry but stopped myself. Crying would have made the whole thing feel disingenuous.

"You need to get out of that house," she said. It felt like my life was starting, or something dramatic like that.

The rest of the weekend went on the same. I realized I could get along so well with the Fog House inhabitants because no one ever put me on the spot or expected more from me than I could give. If I froze up, Julia or Amy would seamlessly change the conversation without making it awkward. Heath spoke in a way that never called for a response, and Vlad simply didn't talk. It was a perfect dynamic.

The house was whimsical and full of eccentric things like empty bird cages filled with vintage baby dolls. Strangely, during the entire weekend, I never once got to watch anyone play that Fog game. I asked Heath about this and she told me that the rituals were private, and I was just a guest.

On Sunday, I packed up, and hugged my new friends. Julia whispered in my ear, "See you soon."

I waved as I drove back out the gravel driveway.

I continued texting Julia after that weekend, about life, stresses, funny moments, and so on. Her messages were much more straightforward than Heath's had ever been, which was a relief. She didn't embellish her texts with asterisks or cryptic language, but still managed to be captivating. She loved making fun of herself and acknowledging the absurdity of her life passion without invalidating any of it. To her, God's existence as a ghost in a video game was an undeniable truth. I was impressed with myself for managing to hold such a powerful person's interest for so long. I drank less during that time.

As the term came to a close, the pressure to make a summer plan was building. I didn't want to be stuck spending those months at my parents' house in Ohio. Julia was fully aware of my situation, and in early May, she texted:

"just live at fh already!!!"

She would pay for everything, and seeing as I didn't have any expendable income or friends, this arrangement sounded like a dream. I told my parents I'd be working on a farm with a schoolmate for the summer. Since they didn't have to worry about my living expenses or dealing with me, I'm sure it sounded like a dream to them too.

Julia and Heath were waiting for me on the porch when I pulled in, holding hands in the moonlight but standing far apart. Julia gave me a hug and Heath went directly to bring in my luggage.

"I'm so excited for you." Julia squeezed my hand. My room was on the second floor, small with faded green wallpaper. There was an empty wooden dollhouse sitting on a white table at the foot of the bed. No people, no furniture. Once I finished unpacking my things in the antique dresser, I came back downstairs, and said hi to Vlad who was eating an apple at the center table and drinking a beer. He nodded at me and I saw then that he looked like he would have called me "faggot" in high school. I found him devastatingly attractive.

A loud bang from the grand piano on the far side of the house rang out and the lights turned off. I jumped back, but Vlad seemed unfazed. I was impressed by how dark it had become. A brooding and complex melody began to play as Heath emerged from a dark hallway with her trademark defeated expression lit by the flickering candle in her hands. Before I could even start to ask what was going on, Heath shushed me. Vlad stood up and approached me, leaving behind his half-finished apple and beer. He put his hands on my shoulders, and I hoped he'd kiss me, or at least hit me. With force, he placed me directly behind Heath, and gave me a tap to follow her.

We marched down another long corridor, the piano echoing through the house. We came to a white door with peeling paint that Heath opened, and a rush of cool air brushed past us. She began to descend a creaking wooden staircase, and I had no choice but to follow, eating a spider web at every step. It was brighter when we reached the concrete landing. A swinging light outlined Heath's black dress, and the bottoms of the pipes that weaved through the ceiling. We turned a corner and passed down another short hall until the room opened to reveal Julia sitting in a circle of cushions. Lit candles and sparkling crystals of varying heights and colors surrounded her. The walls were covered from floor to ceiling with layers of painted paper, and I could faintly make out the impressions of countless gray watercolors, a pair of eyes emerging from every center.

No more music. Vlad pressed down on my shoulder to indicate for me to sit. I felt his hot breath on my neck and thought about how close we were. Heath and Vlad then sat on either side of me, and in a few moments, I heard the creaking of stairs, followed by Amy's emergence from the darkness. She wheeled in a very expensive looking harp, sat it just outside our circle, and began to play.

I might have been a bit scared, but I had also succumbed to the feeling of total acceptance that my fate was now outside of my hands, and maybe that's what I wanted all along. If I died, I at least liked these people. It wouldn't be for such a bad cause.

We all sat on our cushions to the sound of Amy's strings for a while, so long actually, that I was nervous I was supposed to do something to get things going. Just before I embarrassed myself by speaking, an exaggerated, drawn out "Fff" escaped between Heath's lips, maybe for a minute honestly, and then stopped. The harp stopped too.

"Maybe we call her Cathy, but that's not the point." This was Julia now. Her voice was airy and mannered in a way I normally would have minded but didn't. "I've had a lot of fun, lived a lot of lives, but the emptiness, the vast fog, always wins out." Silence. "When I was in my junior year of college, it felt like everything had fallen out from under me, and I hit the ground hard. My life had always been set on a clear path: I was, at all costs, to be an actress. Yet, with every show I did, every time I stepped foot in front of the camera, I felt like I was losing a part of myself. It wasn't that I was bad—people always applauded me. I'm not bragging I'm just being honest," she paused for dramatic effect.

"What once had been my dream, became something evil. I hated watching myself, hated hearing the words come out of my mouth. Hated when people told me I was raw, that I was so real on the stage, because I knew I wasn't. I just knew how to say the words right, I knew how to move my face. I studied, I practiced, and I was good. There's nothing *real* about it." There was disdain in her voice. "I had to stop watching movies or anything that wasn't reality TV. Then I realized reality shows were even more false than scripted work. And I *sobbed* when I watched the Oscars that year, when the actress went up to accept her award, her REward, because she was so happy, she felt like she'd actually done something. That it meant anything." Julia's voice cracked, and she took a breath before continuing. She was so brave.

"Something that seemed so pure and full of hope, a solace for so many, was the world's biggest lie. And I felt like all I was, was a very talented liar." An exhale. "All art became artifice. Every conversation made me nauseous. I would have killed myself but even that felt performative." Heath put her hand on Julia's knee consolingly, but her expression remained blank.

"I dropped out of school and locked myself in my room at my parents', doing nothing on most days. And then one day, after months of agony, my brother brought this game home. It was called 'Fog,' and he found it in a vintage store in Tokyo. You see, he liked to collect eccentric things and thought the cover looked mysterious. And so, we started it up, and slowly realized from the characters and landscape it was supposed to be based on Wuthering Heights on some level." Julia and Amy gave a little laugh, and Julia turned to me. "You'll see how little it actually has to do with the novel." But then she was serious again. She sighed and motioned towards Amy with her head to continue playing, and she did, and I understood then why they always played so much music in church.

"My brother gave up on the game very quickly. I mean, it's a terrible game," she laughed again. "All you do is run around hills, find people with names like Hareton or Linton who are haunted by ghosts, and you kill them. And to find these people, you have to travel outrageously long distances in fog, with nothing to see but the green grass and your running avatar." She paused, then continued. "I had nothing else to do, nothing I *could* do, so I played this game that was so boring, so empty, it felt honest. And I stopped trying to help the people with their ghost problems all together. I just ran through the endless fog. I ran and ran and ran for hours of the day, seeing nothing but the same gray and green. I wondered if I was going crazy, but I couldn't help this feeling that I was searching for something very real."

Heath began a low, deep belly humming, I guess to build to the climax. I had goosebumps by then. "Then, after days of running, I saw her." Vlad started to beat the ground with his palms like a drum, and together they all got louder and louder. "Yes! I saw them—two brilliant, brown eyes, radiating with passion—not animated like the rest of the game, but real!…Alive. In those eyes, I couldn't see a glimmer of artifice." Heath's humming had built into a loud chant and Julia was crying now. I found myself wanting to stand up and cry with her, scream with her. "I knew it was Cathy, the Cathy of Wuthering Heights, her ghost. She had seen how miserable I had become, and wanted to save me because she too knew what it was like to suffer!" Her breath started to shake, "Yes, I was overwhelmed with the sensation that these eyes were the first real thing I had ever seen. Eyes truer than yours or mine. That I was looking at something so much more sublime than simply Cathy. I was staring into the eyes of God." The noises came to a halt, and the room was overtaken by silence again.

"To an outsider, maybe this all seems crazy." I shook my head for some reason. "But why wouldn't this be the exact place where God hides herself? In the endless fog of a made-up world?" I didn't know what I believed, but I knew I'd die for her. "My life began to look better after that. I could bear to read and watch TV, because I had proof. That, although we are all living in the fog, there is still truth buried deep within it." Why did she care so much about truth? "Nothing was perfect. I still felt lost. But there was a semblance of hope that I could find her again, and be free from this prison." Finally, Julia took my hand. "I have invited you, and all of them to join me in my journey. To find that heaven on earth. Please, join us." Everyone clapped and hugged me.

I didn't understand what most of it meant, but I was sold. All I knew was that my life would matter if I helped Julia find Cathy. What was everyone else's excuse?

We went to bed that night right after the ceremony, but, every single other night that summer, we sat and watched Julia play the Fog game for exactly two hours. The ritual around it was always the same: Amy would wheel in her harp, Heath would turn off the lights after the rest of us found seats on the big black couch, and Vlad would light candles and incense on either side of the TV. Julia would take a leather briefcase from a cabinet beneath the TV, open it on the coffee table, and remove a gray PlayStation from it. It would take her a while to plug in the system and turn on the television, but we would respectfully watch in silence.

I surprised myself the first night with how excited I was to see the game in action. Once it finally started up, Amy began playing her harp, and we were met by a gray screen with the word, "FOG," in white bold letters. Below it, there were two options written in Japanese. Julia selected the first, and after we stared at a blank screen for ten seconds, we saw that familiar image of a man in a black overcoat standing on a green hill, the endless fog outstretched before him. Julia let a moment of stillness hang in the air before pressing forward on the controller, and then we all descended together into the fog.

I wasn't exaggerating about the two hours. Even after the first ritual, I was exhausted. It was like the first time I worked at the grocery store—it felt like days had flown by in the span of five minutes. Except in the Fog House, no one could check the clock. We had to sit in the darkness and stare at a screen, waiting for Heath's timer to go off. I was bored out of my mind, thinking maybe all these people really were crazy. My leg started shaking, and Heath silently placed her hand on my knee to stop it. I was paranoid everyone was mad at me for the rest of the night.

The next day, during breakfast, I got a moment alone with Amy, who I felt I could trust. I asked her how she got through that session every night, and she smiled, and told me it was normal to feel the way I did.

"I try to study it like a painting. I look for something new, even in the monotony. For a while I would just daydream as I played the music, but then I realized that the whole experience was much more impactful if I focused."

The next few nights were still pretty tricky, but by the end of the week, I think I understood what she was saying. It became hypnotizing watching that man run through nothingness for two hours straight. When nothing seems to change in the environment except for subtle differences in the density of the fog, hill inclines or declines, and the occasional patch of cobblestone in the grass, you're forced to hone in on every single detail. I started to find the grainy graphics beautiful, like a moving impressionist painting. I mean, those finely pixelated video game graphics were essentially a form of pointillism. I would focus on a tiny corner of the screen and watch the little dots of gray or green barely shift in shade every millisecond like flickering lights. I could even make out blues and purples in the gray if I wanted to.

I became envious of the man in the black overcoat, that his world could be so clear, that his little atoms of air weren't afraid to express themselves. If we could see our own world that way, maybe we'd be more careful about how we existed, how we used every breath, took every step. Even darkness is actually made of billions of living particles. Is that what Julia meant by God? I knew it probably wasn't, but I also could see how this game could start a religion. And I understood why God would choose to hide in such a place, but maybe those were just Julia's words as well.

Weeks went by, and I became increasingly more curious about that two-hour Fog ritual. The day-to-day life we shared was nice but fairly mundane: eating, walking around the property, visiting the horses, listening to the piano. All I could think in the daylight was, "tonight's the night," and I didn't even necessarily mean "the night we find her," just more, another chance at understanding Julia's mind.

The two hours were grueling, for sure, but even the most devout Christians get bored in church sometimes, right? I kept myself entertained by trying to find the space in between the pixels, like maybe I could be a hero and find Cathy there, and everyone would begin to worship me. That if I could just work something out in my head, some little secret, all would be revealed. I decided the fog was a metaphor for the darkness I had been sifting through my entire life, and that Cathy—no, Emily Brontë—had guided me to Julia so I could finally be happy. Yes, it turned out I was special all along, that God had great things in store for me. I could almost forgive my parents for being such aggressive Christians, because, in theory, I understood what it meant to feel God's love, and to love her back.

As time went on, I got closer with my housemates, and began to feel like I was a part of something bigger for the first time in my life. I didn't realize how much I was craving this until I had it, and once I figured out that this sense of community was what had been missing, the thought of ever living without it was devastating. I could never go back to those endless nights of drinking in a dark room in front of a screen, or going to sleep with a stomach ache, picturing my face on someone else's head—someone capable of stringing together coherent sentences.

So, it's understandable why I would try so hard to buy into it. Maybe a month or two in, I finally asked myself if I actually was that committed to my faith or if it was a just story I had to keep repeating so I wouldn't go crazy. I tried to forget the thought ever entered my head, because the good things that came from believing in Cathy far outweighed the bad. I tried with everything I had to convince myself

I was a believer. But there was still that nagging feeling in the back of my mind calling me a liar.

I furiously wrote about it in my journal one evening. Was my problem that I couldn't fully believe in Cathy as God? Was it the same problem that kept me from being the extreme Christian I was born to be? When I thought I finally found something good, I had to break it down like everything else. It felt like expectations were constantly being set in place for me that I was failing, like some big part of my character was missing a solid piece of the human experience of faith, or being able to trust that anything outside of myself meant anything. As much good as the house did, it also validated the one major quality I had always known to be true about myself: that there was something fundamentally wrong with me. And I was still wondering: what came first, the homosexuality or the defectivity? I wasn't sure if that was a word, but I underlined it anyway.

For a long time, I could subdue these feelings of doubt with the post-ritual pink cocktails, but that only got me so far. One day, Amy and I went for a walk in the woods and I thanked her for her advice, and finally asked her how she ended up here. I wanted to know how she *really* felt. She talked about finding the house through an online listing looking for spiritual interns with musical talents. It covered living expenses, and so she figured, "why not?"

"Do you think she'll find Cathy?" I asked.

She smiled and looked down as she pulled aside a thorn bush. "I don't know." She shrugged. "It's nice believing in something though, right? It's not a bad life." We kept walking in silence for a bit. "She's not hurting anyone."

That conversation deeply depressed me.

In early August, Julia recruited me for a project to make an enormous mural. We unfolded yards of canvas on the front lawn in the sun, and painted what felt like billions of dots of gray, white, and black all across it. Occasionally, Julia would use blue or green or a dark purple, but only she could use those exciting colors. We would talk and play music all the while. She asked me about my childhood which she'd never done before, and when it seemed like I was getting uncomfortable, she started telling stories from hers. She was a genius of social interactions in my eyes, but then again, I'm not the best judge. She never once asked me if I actually believed in her God.

After the mural was done and dried in the sunlight, she painted two large eyes at its center, like I expected her to. She hugged me. We hung it up from the balcony in front as a signal to drivers-by that something important was happening in these walls. I could see how proud she was of her creations, both the mural and what it represented. She took my hand and looked in my eyes as she said, "I'm really happy you came." I looked in hers. "I love you, you know that?" I blankly stared, then nodded. That night I drank pink lemonade and vodka until I threw up.

The next day, when everyone was out with the horses, I snuck up to Julia's room on the third floor. I had been there briefly before during my first visit. She had a four-post white bed, with an array of crystals and candles sitting on either side. In the corner of the room was a small statue of a woman with no hands, sitting in the center of a bird bath filled with water. Fresh flower petals floated on the water's surface. Her whimsical decorations seemed dumb and pretentious in light of my hangover.

Heath and Julia slept in separate beds in separate rooms. I don't know if they ever shared a bed, or if Julia was even interested in girls. It made sense that she had a girlfriend either way. There were no family photos anywhere, no evidence that Julia had a life before this religion took it over, and that's exactly how she wanted it. She lived in her own perfect dream world. I resented her then for crying about how miserable her life once was. She didn't deserve to cry in front of us like that, manipulating us to waste hours of our lives to watch her play an excruciatingly boring video game. She was still very much the actress she once had been, and everything about her life was coated in that cloying artificiality she so claimed to hate.

The summer neared its end, and I knew my two choices were to either drop out of college and stay at the house for the rest of my life, or leave the happiest place I'd ever been. The night before I left, we had a picnic like when I first visited. Julia sent Heath out to buy flowers that surrounded our blanket, and Amy played the cello—yet another instrument she was fluent in. We drank a lot and Julia asked each person to go around and say one thing they appreciated about me.

"You don't talk too much," was Vlad's. I blushed.

"Believe in Cathy. Remain open. She will find you." Wasn't really a compliment, but I didn't expect much else from Heath.

"You're thoughtful and can be hilarious when you let yourself be. You're a genuine person." I understood what Julia meant when she said she'd feel sick whenever people told her that her acting was "raw."

Julia was last:

"Whether you believed anything I said or not doesn't matter. What matters is that you let yourself love, and you didn't curl up deeper into yourself to escape. I hope you remember what you learned here for the rest of your life." I gave her a polite smile.

We all continued drinking and laughing. We even got Joseph the caretaker to come out and cheers with us. We fed the horses one last time. Once again, Julia let everyone else clean up while I sat alone with her on the picnic blanket. She swirled the pink liquid in her crystal glass, now tinged orange by the setting sun.

"Do you think you'll come back here?" She didn't look at me as she waited for an answer. I took a sip of my sweet drink.

"I'd really like to." She smiled and gave me a hug, and I let her. She pulled away from me.

"I never wanted to push you more than you were comfortable with. I can read people pretty well, and I knew if I pushed too far, you'd close up." I remained silent. "If me saying I love you made you uncomfortable, I'm sorry. It's just that, I really want you to know that you deserve love." A tear rolled down her face. "We all have struggles we deal with. I know mine can seem so trivial to an outsider. I mean, look at me." She opened her arms as if to motion towards the acres of land and countless possessions that had belonged to her from before she was even born. "But believe me when I say I thought I would die that way, in the darkness." Her voice was getting softer. "When you find something that gives you hope, embrace it like a child, and never let it go." She put her hand on my knee. "This search for Cathy has brought us all together, it's brought us an appreciation for life. A reason to wake up in the morning. What a gift."

"Thank you, Julia." I finished my drink and smiled again. My cheeks hurt.

I paid close attention to her that night during my final Fog ritual. She never showed any impatience with the game. She played with a focused longing, always on the verge of standing to cry with joy, as if at any second, she really would see Cathy. I felt sorry for her.

After everyone went to bed, I left mine with a rolling suitcase and a backpack. I quietly creaked down the stairs, through the corridor of watching gray eyes, into the Fog room. I put down my luggage, and went to the drawer underneath the TV, just making sure I didn't leave anything behind. But alas, all that was there was the leather briefcase.

I unzipped it slowly, and pulled out the PlayStation. I opened the top of the system to reveal the gray Fog (1999) game nestled inside, and realized that was the first time I'd ever seen the physical disk itself. Plain gray with those three bold, white letters. I removed it from the system, and weighed it in one hand. It felt like I was looking down from a skyscraper, short of breath because I wanted to jump. I held it firmly between the fingers of both hands, and slowly let them twist in opposite directions, as if by accident. I didn't think about it while it was happening, it just happened. I heard a crack, followed by the tinkling of small glass fragments falling onto fancy wood. I put both halves into the PlayStation again and closed the top. I placed the system in the briefcase, which I stowed back in its special drawer.

I took my luggage and went out the side door. The August air was almost cool and I found the cicada screeches soothing. I got in my car, a little tipsy still, and drove up the gravel road with my windows down, waving goodbye to the Fog House.

THE PLUMP COUSINS FROM JOHNSON CITY

J.R. Greenwell

I ran toward the house as fast as my skinny seven-year old Appalachian legs would let me, at the same time screaming, "Mama! Mama! We got comp'nee comin' up the lane!" I'd spotted the dust rising above the treetops, nature's way of sending signals into the air of an arrival by someone traveling on the dirt lane dry from the excessive heat in that summer of 1932. "Mama, did'ya hear me?" I slowed to a halt just as the screen door shut behind me.

"I think ever'body in the holler heard'ya. Wonder who'd be comin' to see us? And Lord knows this house is a mess with all this cannin' I've got to git done."

I peered out through the screen. "Looks like a truck," I whispered. It was a rare sight to see a gas-driven vehicle this high in the mountains due to the steep inclines and the deep ruts in the road. Mama stood behind me, and a sense of caution overtook me as I felt her hands gently squeeze my shoulders. We stood there, together, watching as the black truck came closer, the dust cloud rising and tapering off as it neared the fence post not far from our house. As soon as the driver turned off the motor, a woman with bright red lips and shiny auburn hair hopped out on the passenger side of the vehicle, her lavender floral-print dress clinging to her slim body. She started walking toward the house, and then paused.

"Elizabeth!" she yelled. "Elizabeth, are you home?"

Mama stood silent for a few seconds and then she squealed, "Oh my Lord. It's Rita!" She about knocked me down as she opened the door and scampered off the porch. I watched as the two embraced, both weeping. I reckoned they were happy tears as they smiled and laughed as they kept looking at each other, hugging, then looking at each other again, and then hugging some more. I never heard anyone call Mama "Elizabeth" so I figured this woman was someone my mother knew real well.

A rather stout man with thinning hair got out on the driver's side, sweat pouring from his forehead as he wiped it with a handkerchief. His white shirt was almost transparent from the dampness. He wore black shiny shoes. I asked myself, *who wears black shiny shoes when it ain't Sunday?* He said hello to my mama.

Rita and Mama continued to talk over each other when Rita pointed to the back of the truck piled high with boxes and crates. Two of the roundest, palest boys I had ever seen stood up and dismounted. They approached my mama and she hugged them. I suddenly realized that these might be the relatives that my mama and daddy talked about, the ones from Johnson City, somewhere in Tennessee.

Mama looked up to the house. "Brody! Brody Josiah Whitaker, come on out here and meet Aunt Rita and yer cousins!" I stood frozen not sure how to meet these long-lost kin. "Git out here now," she ordered with a hint of nervousness. I opened the door and walked slowly onto the porch and then down the steps, scanning their faces for some kind of friendly gesture to keep me moving forward down the path.

Rita held out her arms and called me over. "Look at you, my little red-headed nephew, and look at those brown eyes, brown eyes as black as coal. I've waited all these years to finally meet you for the first time and put my arms around you." She squeezed me so hard I almost lost my breath. I felt like a mouse being coiled by a snake just before its mouth engulfs the rodent's tiny head and body as it's being slowly swallowed. She smelled good, like nothing I'd smelled before. Maybe a fancy perfume, or a sweet-smelling soap, or perhaps she just smelled good in a natural way. In a quick second I realized the aroma filling my crushed nostrils was a combination of body odor and apple pie. I wanted to lick the melted morsel I spotted on her collar, but she released me before my tongue could touch the fabric.

She introduced me to the stout man with rolled-up sleeves and thinning hair. Fred was his name, and he was her husband. "Why you wearin' black shiny shoes?" I asked. "It ain't Sunday."

He laughed. "The only ones I got." He then leaned over me and said, "No, I got more but your Aunt Rita wanted me to wear my good shoes when we came to visit."

"Oh, Fred," Aunt Rita mockingly responded, "You know that's not true."

He scowled at her. "Yeah, it is."

"And these young boys," Aunt Rita said as she turned around like a cow showing off her newborn calf to the rest of the herd, "are your cousins. This is Junior, and he's twelve, and this one here is my baby boy, Tommy. He just had a birthday last month and he's now ten years old." They looked at me like no one had ever looked at me with frowning eyebrows, terse lips, and noses turned up. "Come on, boys, say 'hello' to Brody." They obliged their mother with a forced smile and a low-volume "hey."

After the introductions, I couldn't remember the cousins' names, as I fixated on the size of these two who were just a tad older than me. Whenever Mama had me select a hen for supper, she always said to pick out the plump one. These two had plenty of plumpness going on. I reckoned city people weighed more than mountain folk did. They even sounded different than me and my mama. Standing next to each other, Mama and Aunt Rita were so far apart with their appearances. Even though Mama was younger than her sister, Aunt Rita looked vibrant and glowing, while mama's face was gaunt and weathered, and even her clothes seemed to just hang on her thin body. I figured city women had it easier than women like my mama.

"Why you dressed like that?" Lil Plump blurted out as he pointed at me.

I instinctively moved over to my mama's side, leaning on her, wondering why he would ask such a question.

"And why are you wearing a pink apron?" Lil Plump's bigger brother, Real Plump asked. His comment left me a bit confused. Was he questioning why I was wearing an apron, or was he objecting to the color?

"Boys, mind your manners," Aunt Rita snapped. "It's cute on him," she said trying to reassure me that she was okay with me wearing my mama's old ratty apron made from floral-print seed bag scraps. "And what are those furry little things you've got on there?"

"Them's rabbits' feet," I explained with excitement. "Mama's been teachin' me how to sew, and Daddy's been showin' me how to clean 'n gut squirrels n'rabbits. When Mama got a new apron from Daddy on her birthday, she give me this one and I fixed it up. Sewed them rabbits' feet 'long the front side and down the edges. 'Waste not want not,' that's what Daddy always says."

"Must be at least two dozen on there, right?" Aunt Rita asked.

"Don't know 'bout how many two dozen is, but each rabbit had four feet and I reckon there's 'bout five or six sets. Heck, I don't know."

"Watch your language young'n," my mama said.

"Yes, ma'am." I looked up to the sky to apologize for my cussing. "Sorry, Lord, for sayin' heck…and then I took these squirrels' tails and sewed 'em on this rag that I'm wearin' on my head, that way I can pretend I got long hair, that is, if I want to."

Aunt Rita touched the fabric on my head. "And did you sew these designs on there too? Looks like mighty fine needlepointing."

"Yes, ma'am. Mama lets me use her special sewin' needle and she gives me any leftover threads after darnin'. Don't know much 'bout needlepointin'. I just sew like I'm darnin' and I make shapes. Them's s'pposed to be stars."

"Boys ain't supposed to sew. That's for girls," Real Plump commented with an air of contempt.

Even before Aunt Rita had a chance to stop her son from throwing one more insult at me, I decided to take matters into my own hands. I looked at Real Plump straight in the eyes and said with certainty, "It don't say it in the Bible that boys cain't sew!"

"You ain't read the whole Bible, and you probably can't read, either."

"Well, I'm learnin' to read, but even if I cain't my mama would've told me if it was in the Bible or not, and she ain't told me. Mama, it ain't in the Bible that boys cain't sew, is it?"

"A'course not, and if it was, I'da fount it by now." Clearly, and as far as I was concerned, Mama was on my side.

Fred wiped his brow again. "Well, looks like we got us a couple of feisty cousins here, don't we?"

"Guess it runs in the family," Aunt Rita chuckled.

Real Plump and I locked eyes as Mama pulled me back. I knew right there and then that I didn't like him, and I sensed the feeling was mutual.

❖

I lived in a sheltered world just outside Raccoon, a small town in Eastern Kentucky, the only child of Elizabeth and Jason Whitaker. My only excursions were to church on Sunday, an occasional trip to Mr. Johnson's general store, and maybe once or twice a year Daddy would hook Jessie up to the wagon and she'd pull us into Pikeville. Sometimes Daddy let me take the reins on the way home. Though our piece of property was not large, I had the run of the countryside with unlimited access to the creeks and hollers that meandered through the mountains. Our house was quite modest, though some might have considered it a shack, but by mountain-folk standards, it was a place for the three of us to call home. There were two rooms in the small house when we first moved in. The front room had a table and two benches, along with the coal stove used for heating and cooking, and there was a backroom where Mama and Daddy slept. Daddy later added a small alcove for me when I got older, separating my space from the front room with only a curtain for privacy, but still ensuring I'd be comfortable in the winter months with heat emitted from the coal stove to warm my chilled bones. Of course, we had a front porch for sitting and chatting after meals, and those times were precious as work and chores dominated most of our days from morning till sunset, and sometimes even later.

But on this day in the summer of 1932, all that tranquility seemed to be threatened. Kin or no kin, I sensed Mama wanted me to do the right thing and share all that was mine. As an only child, I never had to share anything, and now within a short time of their arrival, I would have to give up my most prized possession: my privacy. Mama decided that Aunt Rita would sleep in my bed that evening, and Fred would have the hammock on the porch all to himself where he could oversee the three cousins sleeping in the grass just off the porch. "Kind of like camping out," Fred said out loud when he heard about the arrangements. I had no idea what he was referring to when he made his statement about "camping out." We always slept outside when the nights were warm.

By midday, Mama had made skillet biscuits for our guests, and Aunt Rita had taken sliced ham and what was left of her apple pie out of the truck to share with us. While we ate, Mama and Aunt Rita talked about their mother, Meemaw Allen, and relatives that I had never heard of, those who had died and those who had just run off, never to be heard of again. They even spoke sadly about two brothers who died from the Spanish flu, and three uncles who were killed in battle in the Great War. I listened intensely as they reminisced about their own journeys. Seems that after Meemaw Allen passed away from a strange illness, Aunt Rita and my mama went to live with a distant cousin and her eight kids in Flat Lick, in Harlan County. Soon after that, fifteen-year-old Rita met Fred, and the two of them ran off to Johnson City, leaving Mama behind in Flat Lick. About four years later, Mama met my daddy, who was working in the coal mines, and they got married and moved to Raccoon where my daddy got a job in timber.

Our guests filled themselves with every bit of food that was spread on the table. Soon, Fred fell asleep in the hammock and the Plump Cousins lounged on the edge of the porch. It was a sight to see for sure. I sat alone on the stump in the front yard, pondering how I would spend the afternoon before Daddy came home from work.

"Brody," Mama said as she and Aunt Rita came outside, "why don'cha take the boys up the trail and to the creek 'bove the fork?"

"Mama, do I have to?"

"I think it would be nice fer yer cousins to see the country, to git some fresh air. And anyway, it'll give me and Rita time to start gettin' supper ready 'fore yer daddy gits home later on. Just make sure you're home before yer daddy gits here."

"Yes, ma'am."

Aunt Rita, nudged her sons with her foot. "Yeah, it's time you city boys got a glimpse of how your Aunt Elizabeth and I grew up."

"I've seen enough of it already," Real Plump said sarcastically.

"That's enough," Aunt Rita ordered. "Get off your city-raised behinds and work off some of those vittles you just gulped down."

The Plump Cousins mumbled a few inaudible words, but obliged their mother. It became obvious to me who ruled the roost of this particular side of the family. "And take your shoes off so you don't ruin them in the creek."

As much as I hated leading my cousins into an afternoon of exploration and adventure, I knew my mama would want me to show my manners and do what she asked of me. Without saying a word, I gathered my walking stick and my leather pouch for collecting rocks, and I started to walk. I didn't look back. I figured they would follow me, or maybe not. The Plump Cousins, both barefooted, quickly caught up with me.

As we meandered up the trail, I could hear the giggles and the under-the-breath comments about what I was wearing, my red hair, and the way I was walking. More than once I heard them say "sissy boy." I paid it no mind; however, the occasional pebble hitting the back of my legs was starting to annoy me, but I moved on. After a short time or so, Lil Plump started to whine that he was tired, so we sat a spell just to cool off. We perched on the big rocky ledge under the shade of a couple of yellow poplars next to Mr. Yancy's cleared meadow. The field was full of wildflowers, especially Queen Anne's Lace.

Lil Plump seemed taken by the blooms in the field. "Look at all those flowers out there. I wanna pick some for Mama."

"Pick all you want on the way back. Pick 'em now and they'd be dead before we got home," I said with authority.

We started hiking up the ridge. The trail got steeper and narrower, and occasionally I'd look back to see if they were keeping up. Their faces were as red as pickled beets stuffed into one of Mama's canning jars, but they were keeping pace with me. The best spot for wading was high on the ridge, where the shallows moved quickly and the water was cool and refreshing, so the extra effort to get there was well worth the long hike. Just before we reached the top of the ridge, we could hear the rapids. My excitement grew as we neared the waters. Before I could even tell them to be careful, both my cousins stripped down and entered into the stream. I sat on the edge with my feet in the water, tending to the boys as if I were the eldest and watching out for their safety. I gazed at the clouds drifting overhead, trying to anticipate the amount of moisture that was being carried over the land to some unknown destination. I watched a couple of crows attacking a red-tailed hawk as they were obviously fighting over territory. I smelled the freshness of the water as it splashed against my feet. After a short time of day dreaming, I heard a shift in tone from laughter to grizzly groans of pleasure. I look to my left to see my older cousin on the edge of the water beating a small turtle with a large stone.

I ran over to him as quickly as I could, anger boiling over in my small body. "What are you doin'!" I screamed.

"I killed it," Real Plump bragged.

I looked down on the bleeding carcass, a tiny turtle no bigger than my fist, its shell shattered. It had no idea its demise would be coming at the hands of a city dweller. I turned to face my cousin, and I spread my legs in a stance to give me more support as I was about to launch into a fit of rage. I gritted my teeth and stared so hard at my cousin that I could feel my temples hurt. I suddenly remembered I promised my mama and daddy that I would never fight. Not anyone, but they never said I couldn't get angry. "You'll pay for this!" I yelled as I picked up the tiny victim.

"It's just a turtle," Real Plump yelled back at me. "Why you acting so crazy and all?"

"It's a sin to be evil, and what you just did was evil. My daddy said we only kill what we need to eat." For a second, I envisioned holding my cousin down and forcing him to take a bite of his victim just so he could justify the murder, but that would probably be the end of me. I certainly wasn't afraid of him, but Real Plump was older and larger. Instead, I walked over to where the boys had piled their clothes, and without even thinking twice, I tossed their britches and shirts into the stream. There was a brief moment of silence as we watched their clothing bob and weave down the rapids and out of sight.

"Look what you did!" Lil Plump hollered.

"Guess you'll have to go git 'em. I'm heading back to bury this dead turtle. To git home, take the stream down to the fork and then cross over the meadow where the flo'ers are. It's a shortcut to the house." After I'd taken a few steps, I turned around and said, "Don't forget to pick some flo'ers fer yer mama, and oh…watch fer them bears." I just added that last bit about the bears to make them little more apprehensive about being alone in the mountains. I scampered down the path, leaving the cousins on their own.

I made it past the fork and then around the bend. I dug a shallow grave on the side of the path and buried the tiny turtle. I said a makeshift Evangelical prayer that Preacher Thompson would be proud of. I even started singing "When the Roll Is Called up Yonder," but ended up only humming the tune when I realized I didn't really know all the words. I was sure God would forgive me.

I decided to wait for the cousins on the edge of Mr. Yancy's meadow. My temper had eased up a bit, and I figure that I should at least get them back to the house. My Mama would expect that of me. If the boys took my advice they'd be walking through the field within the hour or so, and if not, they'd be walking on the main road. Either way, I wouldn't miss them. I lay down atop the ledge under shade of the yellow poplars, and I drifted off into a quiet sleep, my walking stick across my chest.

I was awakened later by the sounds of whimpering boys. I looked up to see the Plump Cousins, without their clothes, walking barefoot and gingerly through the briars separating Mr. Yancy's meadow and the lane. Lil Plump clutched a bouquet of Queen Anne's Lace in one hand as he tried to maneuver through the thorny canes with the other. Real Plump wasn't doing any better with two hands. I sat and watched knowing how painful it must have been, but *it was terrible what happened to the turtle as well* I told myself. They finally made it through the thicket and walked right by me as they seemed to know the way to the house and didn't want my help. I got up and followed them. Their backsides were sunburned, and their arms, legs and feet bled profusely from the trip through the briars. Walking behind them, I marveled at how round they were. Most people in the mountains were lean and thin. These two looked like they were ready to be put into the oven and roasted for a Sunday dinner. Of course, and without an oven, the two were already half baked from the long exposure to the sun, especially that part of the body that never even sees the light of day.

We finally made it to my lane and the closer we got to the house, the louder their wails became. I saw Aunt Rita on the porch waving to her children, glad to see them, and then suddenly her face showed her terror as she saw their naked red skin and bleeding limbs. Aunt Rita opened her mouth, stretching her red lips as far as she could, then screamed as any mother in distress would have. Fred, still in the hammock, raised his head and squinted his eyes in disbelief. Mama and Daddy came running from around the back of the house. I felt a sense of uncertainty come over me and I suddenly realized what I had done was terribly wrong, especially when Daddy made eye contact with me.

Even with all the pain he was enduring, Lil Plump raised the weedy white blossoms in the air and yelled out to his mother, "Look, Mama! I brought you some flowers!"

❖

Aunt Rita and Mama brought bed linens out to the yard to cover the boys' naked bodies. Without hesitation, Mama turned into a nursemaid, fetching soap and water, and then lard and kerosene. Once the boys' wounds were cleaned, Aunt Rita applied the lard to the boys' backsides to ease the pain caused by the sun, then the two women applied the kerosene to the briar wounds to keep out any infection. The application of the flammable liquid only made the Plump Cousins suffer more, and their pleas to stop went unheeded.

"Son," my daddy said, "we need to talk." He led me to the side of the house and I sat down on the woodpile. He took a deep breath. A really long breath. It was never a good sign when Daddy took a long breath before he spoke.

"S'plain to me what happened with them boys."

"Well," I said, feeling the presence of his towering body above me.

"You know to tell me the truth…"

"Yes, sir." My mouth was so dry but I didn't dare ask for water. "We went up to the ridge to git to the stream, and the boys went swimming…and…"

My daddy was no fool, and I knew he wasn't buying my short side of the story by the way he furled his brow. "Yep," he said, "let's make this easy before you go any deeper. Them boys got wet, and you didn't. Them boys are sunburnt, and you ain't. Them boys are cut up to high heavens with briar barbs, and you ain't. Now s'plain that to me."

I told my daddy how my cousins went into the water, and then the oldest cousin killed a turtle with a stone, and I got angry. "Daddy, I got so mad I wanted to hurt him, and then I remembered my promise to you and Mama, never to fight, so I decided I'd git even with him."

I didn't even have to tell Daddy the following details, as he rolled them off one by one as if he had been there, even about the chiggers. "When I saw that boy clutchin' them Queen Anne's Lace, I knew they'd been in Mr. Yancy's meadow, and we both know when the lace is out, so is the chiggers, right?"

"Yes, sir, that's right. But the young'n, he wanted some flowers."

"Did you tell 'im 'bout the chiggers?"

"No sir. He prob'bly don't even know what they is."

"Well, I reckon he'll know by sunrise...and all the way on the ride to Louisville."

"Louisville?"

"Yep. They's leavin' in the mornin' to head to Louisville. You see son, all your Aunt Rita's fam'ly has is what they got in that truck of theirs. That's it. That's all they got."

"I thought they's rich."

"Hardly. Seems Fred's business went under with the depression hittin' the country. They's movin' in with his fam'ly in Louisville. We might not e'er see 'em ag'in."

"That's sad, Daddy. That's real sad."

My daddy took another deep breath. "Son, you might've thought your kept yer promise to me and yer mama, but in reality, you didn't. You just fought in a differ'nt kind a way. A man can do as much damage with his mouth and his mind as he can with his fist. You was angry with yer cousin, but did'ya think that maybe he was angry, you know, about leavin' his home, his friends, even his way of life?"

"No, sir, I didn't. I didn't know."

My daddy paused for a moment. I could see he was thinking, and thinking really hard. "Hear them boys still cryin'?"

"Yes, sir, I do."

"You know what'cha gotta do to make it right, don'tcha?"

"Yes, sir, I do."

"Well come on. I'll go with ya."

"You ain't gonna take the strap to my backside?"

"Nope, not this time. Not this time."

I followed my daddy's lead as we headed to the front yard and down the lane. I turned to see my mother standing on the porch, a pan in her hand, probably our supper upon our return. My daddy didn't say much as we turned the corner to head to the fork. I could hardly keep up with his long strides. I grabbed his hand to slow him down. He stopped and looked at me.

"Daddy, I need to know somethin'."

"What is it?"

I was almost embarrassed to ask, but I needed to know. "What is...what is a sissy boy?"

"Why you need to know that?"

"Just wonderin', I guess."

Again, Daddy took his time to answer my question. "Well. I reckon it's a boy who kind of takes after his mama. Sometimes a boy will outgrow it. Sometimes, he don't."

"Is bein' a sissy boy a good thing or a bad thing?"

"Well, probably neither, but I'd have to say it would depend on who yer mama was, right?"

Daddy chuckled for a second, probably surprised with his own clever response. I smiled too at his willingness to be honest with me. I guess he had to be open with me with God watching and all. "Daddy…"

"Yep?"

"I want to go on my own. I need to do this myself. I know 'zactly where them clothes are. Round the bend. It ain't far."

"Well, son…"

"I need to do it. I would feel better if I did it myself. Them cousins gonna need them clothes." I didn't even wait for his permission as I darted down the path to the bend. Winded and spent, I ran past Mr. Yancy's meadow and took the longer way to the stream. I finally reached the calm waters, and there in the bend were my cousins' britches and shirts, hung up in the stones along with other creek debris. I gathered them and made my way back home.

❖

The sun was beginning to set as I neared my home. The sky was more orange than usual, or maybe I had never noticed it before, but somehow it was different. Even I felt different. Somebody, probably my daddy, had built a small fire in the front yard. I heard voices. The crying had been replaced with laughter. I walked slowly toward the small fire surrounded by my cousins, my family. As I approached them, they became quiet. I walked over to Real Plump and Lil Plump and gave them their clothes.

"They's a little wet, but I reckon they's clean," I said apologetically. I heard Aunt Rita giggle.

"Thanks," the Plump Cousins responded in unison.

"I'm real sorry I threw yer clothes in the stream. And I'm sorry I told you to go through Mr. Yancy's meadow. I knew you'd be pickin' up chiggers and get cut up in the briars. It was mean of me, and I'm sorry."

Aunt Rita cleared her voice. "Junior, you got something to say to Brody?"

"Yes, ma'am." He stood up and looked me in the eyes. "I'm sorry I killed your turtle. That was mean of me."

Tommy stood up next to his brother. "I'm sorry I called you a sissy boy. I wasn't really making fun of you. Junior made me say it."

"I did not!"

Fred had to add his two cents. "It doesn't matter who said what. So why don't you boys all shake hands so we can get some supper."

It was awkward as we tried to shake hands, something I had never done before. For some reason I felt the urge to hug Junior, so I did. He hugged me back. Tommy did the same thing. "And anyway," Tommy said, "if we hadn't gone through the field, Mama wouldn't have gotten those flowers!" Seemed like everyone laughed.

Mama walked over and gave me one of those mama hugs that I always liked getting. "So proud of you, Brody, and I know God is too." She leaned over and whispered in my ear, "Don't be worryin' 'bout the chiggers. I washed them boys down with a good 'mount of kerosene. I eg'spect they's legs would catch on fire before any chiggers had a chance to dig in." A few minutes later, she filled plates with green beans and corn cooked with smoked hog jowls, and before we ate, Daddy said the blessing as well as any preacher might do. We all sat around the fire enjoying each other's company and conversation, and of course, Mama's good cooking.

I learned a lot on that hot summer day in 1932. In the flickering glow of the fire, I listened to my daddy and Fred talk about the coal war going on in Harlan County, the depression, the upcoming election, and the hard times falling on most of the country. Fred kept saying, "And if I hear one more time that things are going to get better, I'll spit," and then he'd wipe the sweat from his forehead. I suddenly realized the nervousness in Aunt Rita's laughter as she shielded her emotions behind her red lipstick, and the bravery she needed to keep her family together, especially in the hard and uncertain times facing them ahead. And in the next few hours, I bonded with the only cousins I knew. Tommy even agreed to write me letters after they settled down in Louisville, and I promised I'd write him back. I even gave Junior and Tommy each a rabbit's foot right off my apron for good luck on their trip.

But the biggest revelation for me that day was finding out I was a sissy boy. That's right, pure and simple, an Appalachian sissy boy. Though the life of any sissy can be complicated, to say the least, I would never be bothered by the term used as a misogynist slur when it was thrown my way. I affectionately and proudly embraced the description as a term of endearment that honored the person I most adored, my mama. Sure, I respected my daddy, but like most Appalachian women, she was firm, yet caring; determined, yet flexible; and most of all, she was the foundation of our family. While my daddy worked in timber and other odd jobs, it was Mama who walked behind Jessie, our horse, with a plow strap hanging tight around her shoulders preparing the soil to get the year's crops planted. She was the one who cooked and canned, each jar containing the intense amount of labor it took to bring seeds to fruition to make sure we had enough to make it through the next winter. She milked the cow, churned the butter, collected the eggs, fed the livestock, prepared meals and cleaned on a daily basis. She washed clothes by hand in the nearby creek. She tended to me when I was sick, listened to me when I had questions, and most importantly, she gave me a firm grasp of morality to know the difference between right and wrong. Even when I often doubted the existence of a god, which was often, she was right there telling me that I'd go to Hell if I kept having those thoughts.

The next morning at dawn, Aunt Rita, Fred, and my cousins got into their truck and left. Daddy went to work without saying a word, and Mama cried all day while she finished canning green beans. I wanted to help her but she said she needed to be alone.

I sat by myself on the porch with Mama's special sewing needle and a few strands of her darning thread, and I sewed make-believe stars on my apron, one for each of my cousins I would probably never see again. Occasionally, I looked up to scan the tree tops lining the lane, hoping to hear a black truck or see a trail of dust heading my way. Not sure why, but I cried too.

GUEMES GETS AWAY

John Whittier Treat

"Blow it up with dynamite. Derek has some in his shed from when he put in his big dock."

Greg had walked into the meeting late and didn't know what in the world anyone was talking about. A note in his mailbox this afternoon informed him there was an all-island meeting tonight at the General Store, agenda undisclosed. He'd decided to walk instead of taking the jeep, still curious after four months here what he might yet discover along the road. It was late March and it would be dark on his way home, so he'd been delayed looking for his flashlight, not sure where it was or even if he had unpacked it yet. Boxes from his move up here still lay scattered around the house.

The room erupted in laughter, but nervous laughter as if no one knew if the hoarse male voice had been kidding or not. Greg had come because he was curious about what kind of neighbors he had, not knowing anyone yet, as well as about what was so goddamn important all of a sudden.

"Shit, Hank, that crap has to be ten years old. Wouldn't blow up your ass, much less the ferry." More laughter. That must be Derek, Greg figured, while wedging himself into a chair around one of the little café tables. He joined two women and another man also holding a flashlight.

"Hell," bellowed a woman standing in the front of the room, looking as if she'd appointed herself in charge. "A lot of good sinking the ferry will do. If half of you have your own boats to go back and forth, then so do the weekend folks, ferry or no ferry." She extracted a pencil from her hair bun and scribbled on the small pad of paper she held in her hand.

Greg was entertained by the room's salty language when it dawned on him, listening to the hubbub around him, that everyone was arguing about whether to close off the island from anyone additional coming over, now that this China flu was headed this way up from Seattle. Jesus, he swore to himself, I'm brand-new here and there's already a health crisis. Guemes residents had been summoned to discuss what measures to take against the coronavirus. He'd moved to Seattle from the east coast decades ago to skirt one epidemic and now, in an even more remote corner of the country, loomed another. That's why they were crowded into the G.S., which was what everyone called the General Store, the only real business on the island. It had the basic foodstuffs, a good selection of wines, the local newspaper, a seating section that served simple meals, and three gas pumps out front. These were the amenities that made living here imaginable for Greg, so far. For anything else you had to take the small ferry across to Anacortes and walk, bike or drive from there.

"Look," said a blond woman with two equally blond children squirming in her lap, "We need that ferry as much as anyone else. It's already running on a reduced schedule and this morning I had to wait for two to go and come back before there was room for us third time around. One of my girls had a dentist's appointment and we missed it."

Feeling the parvenu, he looked about trying not to be obvious. G.S. was a handsome building, better than what Guemes needed or deserved: sturdy pillars, fine wood paneling, large double-paned windows, and art on the walls. There was a little stage for musicians to perform on. Whoever designed and built this had lavished love and money on it. The two girls who worked the evening shift behind the counter stood ready to sell anyone an espresso drink, or any of the three stale pastries left in the glass display case next to them.

He had no more than a nodding acquaintance with these girls. He'd just moved to the island. For over a decade now he'd rented the same house for the occasional weekend to bring a series of semi- and full-boyfriends to it: Sean, Mike, Dave, Jesús, Steve. When the owners told him they were putting the house on the market, he headed them off and bought it with cash. He hadn't parted with his condo in Seattle, though he was beginning to fix it up in anticipation of the day he would.

The only reason he hadn't yet was his indecision whether this move to the smallest of the San Juan Islands was going to be permanent.

The islanders crowded into the G.S. debated what to do. There wasn't one case of the virus on Guemes, and no one had heard of anyone with symptoms. But any cough in the room raised the level of tension. The average age, he surveyed, was way up there. People were worried if not yet scared. Island Hospital was across the water in Anacortes, but who knew if they had those special ventilators.

"Can the store get any of those face masks?" asked Marjorie, the sole black person in the room. He knew her name already because she was quasi-famous: she had written successful mystery novels set on the island, and copies were always for sale in the G.S. His eyes scanned the store's shelves: Marjorie's novels, imported pasta, tuna in glass jars, Belgian chocolates, Perrier water; but no masks.

"Should we start wearing them?" Marjorie asked. "No one here has one on. But wouldn't we, if we had some?"

In time it was decided by murmured consent that the island would post a polite notice—"Marjorie, you're a good writer!"—on the island's Facebook page and the General Store's website that part-time residents should think of staying away for "the duration."

His fellow islanders rose from their seats and were mingling. He was quick to exit before anyone else. He stood in the gravel lot on the far side of the gas pumps and watched the last ferry of the night pull into the landing. The several cars on its deck switched on their headlights, and a young woman mounted the horse that had come over with them.

He noticed the first vehicle in line for the return trip to Anacortes next morning. Someone meant to get a head start on everyone else by leaving his van in place overnight. Someone who was eager to get home or get away from home. *Guemes get-away. Guemes gets away*, he thought, amused by his pun. Good title for Marjorie's next thriller.

Walking down the road to the water, ripples from the just-docked ferry still lapped against the bulwark made of logs and tar. He shoved his hands into his pockets and watched the cars, then the horse, unload. When the two ferrywomen chained the boarding ramp and strolled to their nearby autos, he took the flashlight out of his coat and headed back. Irene was outside the darkened store, speaking loudly to another woman and remonstrating with her hands. He was glad not to have been the last to leave the meeting.

On his walk home one van going his direction passed him with a wider berth than usual. The driver flashed his high beams, an island way of signaling hello and goodbye at the same time. Greg waved his flashlight over his head to return the greeting.

In his house he sat at his small desk and checked his email. One of the reasons he had bought this house was that it had a good internet connection, though he knew that he could have arranged good internet anywhere on the island. This house, a snug two-story modern affair, the only one like it on the island, had all the comforts of home. It had a history, albeit a brief one. Everyone he'd come with here had been a short fling aside from Steve, the major upgrade he thought was going to be it for life. All of them moved away, drifted apart, or were just gone. Now he was here alone. Two people, he recalled, had been perfect in this house. The time he tried three, it was clearly one too many. Everyone had had to be careful not to embarrass themselves or another. But by all by himself? Spacious. Up the metal spiral staircase was the one real bedroom, and a combination office/guest room.

He sat at the desk staring at the screen. He skipped the messages from list-serves he hadn't unsubscribed from yet. He clicked the bookmark for the Guemes Island's Facebook page, nestled between bookmarks for the *New York Times* and the *Seattle Gay News*. He didn't find any warnings for the world to stay away. That said here, if nowhere else, was an island free of contagion and determined to stay that way.

❖

When Greg was a boy the terror was polio. He had few memories of it, but he did recall the fear. He remembered March of Dimes cards, into whose slots kids inserted dimes until full, when the teacher or the usher at the movie theater would take it. He recalled his classmate Arthur, who had one leg shorter than the other, wrapped in a heavy metal brace.

Polio epidemics were a twentieth-century phenomenon, and each was worse than the last. His parents were petrified by it. He remembered when people practiced social distancing without calling it that. Social distancing meant not going over to Jimmy's house for his birthday party; it meant not being allowed to take swimming lessons at the YMCA for two summers in a row. It meant seeing a president in a wheelchair on the cover of an old *Saturday Evening Post* magazine and knowing not to ask what had happened to him. Twice he stood in long lines at his elementary school. The first was for an injection; a few years later, a sugar cube with a pale spot on the top. And that was that. No more polio, except in Africa. That was when everyone believed if penicillin didn't cure you, something else would come along soon that would. Dr. Sabin and Dr. Salk were great men. He read about them in the *Weekly Reader* they got at school.

In the nineteen-fifties there was one thing that horrified him. Iron lungs. He saw photos of them in magazines. Long metal tubes anchored to trollies, with an opening at only one end and once in it there was no escape. He wasn't clear on what they were for, but he panicked at the sight. One day he'd feel weak in his legs and the next thing he knew they'd come, take him away and insert him in one, never to be free again to run, get into fights, play stick ball with his friends, sit at the dining room table with his parents, or even go to school. It would be the ultimate quarantine. He would live out his feeble days, and not that many of them, without ever touching another person. He would never be a soldier, have a girlfriend, or be the first man on the moon.

❖

The next day the weather was clear and warm for March. Greg walked to the beach.

Not everyone on Guemes was the retired rich, or even the working comfortable. By the look of most of the houses, many with sheds or barns long past being useful, many of his neighbors were just scraping by. Best anyone knew the Samish had been here originally. They camped on Guemes in the winter. The island had a fresh water spring on it. The British sailed past it but the Spanish named it in honor of a Viceroy of Mexico at the end of the eighteenth century. By the end of the nineteenth, the U.S. government had seized the spring and sent everyone else packing.

One of the houses he passed, ramshackle and empty, its windows covered with plywood, had a holiday wreath hanging from its front door half obscured with weeds. Christmas was months before but the wreath looked fresh from where he stood. Must be artificial, he concluded. Plastic. Fake greenery on an island covered with the real stuff. Guemes had trees and ferns erupting in the understory larger than anything he'd seen in Seattle's parks. But when things are severed from their roots they die, and so some absentee owner had bought this wreath at the K-Mart or Ace Hardware in Anacortes for his derelict property's festive, long-term decoration.

Potlatch Beach was deserted. He would have been surprised if it were otherwise. Not only was it still late winter, but this was not a beach anyone came to for fun. It was all boulders and rocks and little eddies with faint proofs of life, botanical and zoological, clinging to wet surfaces. He made his way to where the boulders began to sink below the receding tide and balanced himself atop one of the largest. He stretched his arms out as if he were Rio's Christ the Redeemer, either bidding welcome or farewell to whoever might spot him. He took a deep breath and was reminded of why he might stay in Guemes for good: the air, having encountered no land since Asia that was as clean as he was ever going to breathe. Somewhere in China right now, people were tethered to oxygen tanks and breathing machines, *ventilators*, maybe even iron lungs if desperate enough for the next breath and lucky as well. But by the time weather arrived it was cleansed of germs and toxins by storms and gales, cleansed free of pollutants by the mountains between the island and the open Pacific.

He heard someone approach, the solid sound of a man's heavy boots on rocks, the same sound he must have made a few minutes earlier when there was no one to hear. The man was about ten years older than he was and handsome in a way that he could appreciate. He was like the high school soccer coach a gay kid would have a crush on before he knew what a crush on another man was, but now it's decades later and he sees him again. The face was strong if lined; the nose and chin the most prominent features; the hair in place if gray at the temples; short wide sideburns; the eyes deep-set and narrow but dark blue pupils evident even at a distance; clean-shaved but with the dark, virile trace of a beard that would sprout back by the end of the day; lips sealed in an enigmatic smile.

The stranger was wearing a heavy parka and corduroy pants as well as leather work boots. He stayed on his rock some fifty feet away, large hands resting at his side until he raised one to shield his eyes, looking out at the same horizon Greg had been surveying. He nodded, aiming with care. Fifty feet suited Greg's shyness just fine. The return nod did nothing to dissuade him of the notion he might have just found his own kind on Guemes. Steve, his last boyfriend, had had a similar look, that former-soccer-coach-now-a-lawyer one. With Steve, he indulged his new fondness for men a bit older than himself. Just as his own countenance had long eased into daddy territory, he found himself drawn to the same.

But Greg was not going to speak with the soccer coach any more today than he might have in line at the G.S. It wasn't the new excuse of social distancing that kept one from making his way over to the other; it was the rock and boulder-strewn beach, which any effort to cross would have had either of them looking too eager to connect. *No, that's not quite true*, he admitted. A man this handsome, and who had been around for as many years as he estimated, was sure to possess a past that included other men, lovers found and lost, maybe someone he cared for but no longer alive. He was likely to be positive, like Steve had been: both lucky enough to have made it to safe ground when the cavalry arrived. None of that would have been part of their first conversation, of course, but soon enough it would have been; and Greg was not eager for it. So much of it would be rote.

So he concluded, on the basis of no evidence, that he and the soccer coach were both AIDS widowers, though technically he was not. Steve had died a normal way, if a bit young for it: a heart attack on the squash court, a brief ambulance ride to the emergency room, and then the news that only if the doctors had been able to get to him sooner. But their relationship had always been a threesome, the virus never far away, and he would always wonder if a negative lover not subsisting on the meds might have been able to play squash at the age of forty-five without collapsing.

He and his soccer coach. *Here we are, washed up on the rocky shores of a remote island, next stop Siberia.* They were, he suspected, here for the long stay now; and he decided just that moment, without thinking through all the consequences, that he would stay on Guemes. Trips to Seattle, and they were sure to happen, would be the weekends away from home that this island had been for a decade. Wherever the soccer coach hailed from—San Francisco, Boise, Tampa—he was here now, and sooner or later he and Greg would initiate a conversation briefly awkward—at the gas pumps, on the ferry, somewhere—which would continue until the whole ball of string had unraveled and until there was nothing to say that the other hadn't already said, or was just about to.

He decided to head back from the beach, but hesitated whether he should wave goodbye to his distal companion when he next looked his way. He chose not to, and stepped down from his boulder. *You can be lonely anywhere*, he comforted himself, *not just on an island.*

❖

Greg checked the island's website and saw that the "town council" had declared a travel ban. He was not aware that Guemes was a town, or that it had a council. No outsiders, bold red letters announced, were permitted to arrive by ferry, and since there was no other public transportation, that was that. By the next day the website for the Anacortes newspaper reported the same, and added as a late-breaking development that the Washington State Attorney General had rescinded the ban as illegal.

When he drove to the G.S. for groceries, which he didn't really need but was curious about recent developments, the place was abuzz. The owner of the store, he overheard, was trying to reach the Attorney General in Olympia for clarification, so far with no success. He picked up a pound of ground Peets Coffee, a bag of unsalted roasted cashews, two bottles of chardonnay and lined up at the register. One of the girls he knew was working, though it wasn't her usual shift. He listened to what she was saying over the shoulder of a man in front of him.

"They're saying someone on Orcas has got it. A Vietnamese guy who just came back from a trip there." Greg half-joked, loud enough for everyone to hear, that the store had better start stocking facemasks after all, but he realized that his voice sounded anxious, not funny.

"Can't get 'em. Everyone's out," a voice behind him said. "Even Wal-Mart."

On the way back to his house he thought, not for the first time, how human beings believe they'll be the ones to escape, stay ahead of trouble, avoid viruses as if they flee. He had left New York when people were getting sick; now, on Guemes, about as far as away as one could get in the Lower Forty-Eight, he was among folks who were betting a short stretch of water would keep them safe. *Doesn't work that way*, he said to no one but himself.

The last time he and Steve had screwed was here on Guemes, one Saturday afternoon, in the rental house that he now owned. Steve had had occasional health issues. Things were going wrong for him that shouldn't for a man his age, and eventually something would get him but that was true for everyone. They were both aware the clock was ticking without ever mentioning it. Steve, a veteran of the bad old days, had never dumped his supply of barbiturates, and made sure Greg knew where they were in his apartment. But of all the things that had gone wrong, Steve's libido wasn't one of them. When they fucked that last weekend, Greg was glad as always there were no neighbors close by to hear. He joked once more with Steve *there better be an undertaker on the island, should things go too far*, "too far" never defined because that would ruin the mood.

Late summer sun streamed through the bedroom window. The electric fan whirled. Two birds bickered atop the skylight. A half-squeezed tube of lube lay on the floor. One leg slid atop another, one soft belly rubbed against the next. No restraint. Two hands grasp a neck, another two the buttocks. No mask. An arched back, clenched toes, two tongues at work in different places. No condom. One finger followed by two. No caution. A head of ruffled curls, a chest covered with damp fur. No dining in restaurants. A wince, a smile, familiar pain, then the boyish giggle. Maintain social distancing. A whiskery chin in a crack, a swelling cock wedged between pecs. No touching your face. Touching each other's face. Cover your mouth when you cough. *Pound me.* Use disinfectant. No virus. *Fuck me.* Take your temperature every day. A virus. *Wreck me.* Wash your hands for twenty seconds. *Use me.* Don't listen to what the TV says. *Breed me.* Don't read the newspapers. *I love you.* Stay home unless you are essential.

Someone on Guemes got through on the phone to the State Attorney General. But soon everyone had a different idea of what he said they could or couldn't do with their island in the middle of a pandemic.

❖

Greg sat in the Adirondack chair he dragged out of the storage shed on his property because he had willed today's weather to be warm enough for it. Optimistically he'd put on a short-sleeved shirt. He brought out his laptop and listened to a Vancouver internet station play classical music through its tinny speaker. He chuckled when he thought how his neighbors thought they could keep the coronavirus at bay. That, by moving here, or by not moving if this is where they were from, they would keep disease away like the other things they didn't like: traffic, airplane noise, illegal aliens, air pollution, homosexuals. He looked up and saw birds flying overhead in a tight formation. They are returning from somewhere south, and he had to wonder what they might be bringing with them.

A voice came over the radio to interrupt the music for a brief news update at the top of the hour. It was Canadian news, not American. No cases reported in Alberta yet.

People always think they can escape. Many times they do. He had gotten away from New York, its rising rents and restaurant prices, his friends either dead or on a conveyor belt rolling that way. A traveler can prepare for new places by reading up on them, and Greg had, but nothing prepared him for that first breath of air when he got off the plane. The Pacific Northwest smells like spring, yearlong, at least for part of each day. The Northwest had clean air, it had space to spread out, it had fresh fish, it had wild blackberries, it had snow-capped mountains even in summer. What it didn't have, or so Greg thought for his first few naive months, was obnoxious crowds, corrupt politicians, persistent mosquitoes, state income taxes; it did not have the Ku Klux Klan, it did not have queer-baiters, and it did not have AIDS until it did. He tested negative after arriving, so he hadn't added to the demographic, but it was here. It lurked, disguised itself, prowled at night, concealed in the daylight, kept quiet at all times; but it was here. Through Steve's eyes he would see it everywhere, as if he had donned magic glasses.

The news bulletin over, Mozart followed Bach followed Mahler. When his laptop lost its internet connection—the signal was weak outdoors—he didn't bother to reconnect. He stayed in his Adirondack chair—stylish in the Northeast but maybe the only one on Guemes—because the sun had moved enough to award him with warmth. He fell asleep with the sound of birds, just returned, chirping atop his trees as if seeing old friends after a long time away.

❖

A newcomer is always an awkward person to be, a potential boon or a burden. He starts out as a stranger, maybe the scout for an invading tribe, a solitary exile from his own people, a wealthy man with an ill-gotten fortune to invest, or a lost soul left by God to perpetually wander. *Be not forgetful to entertain strangers: for thereby some have entertained angels unawares.* From the Bible. Leviticus, of all places. He had to laugh. He wasn't a religious person, but that verse had stuck with him, just like Blanche's last line in *Streetcar* had.

Guemes was so small that new arrivals were apparent to everyone and freely interrogated. *Seattle, yes. No, before that New York, and before that here and there in New England. No, years, decades ago. A family? No, all by myself.* After that last, inevitable query the number of further questions always decreased, because so much else could be assumed, and in his case, with good reason.

On Friday he had to take the ferry into Anacortes for his prescriptions. Hypertension, depression; PrEP, of all things. For him. Living on Guemes Island for God's sake. Who was he kidding.

There were always other islanders at the Rite Aid, but being on the mainland meant everyone assumed the cloak of usual Northwest diffidence while in line. Folks who on the ferry might ask the purpose of his excursion would never do so here. This time the Rite Aid had a piece of paper taped to its automatic sliding glass doors. Reduced hours. A request that customers observe the new rules. But at drug stores, customers always stand at a remove from each other while waiting for refills. *Please stand here to insure your and others' privacy.* Okay, sure, no problem. Social distancing, already long-time standard practice in drug stores. He stood at measured lengths between two truly ancient senior citizens with his multivitamins, a box of Band-Aids and a plastic jug of Listerine in hand; innocent purchases—things that healthy and *normal* people need—among which to hide his guilty one.

On his way out of the pharmacy, his cover purchases in a plastic bag and the pointless one with other vials in a smaller paper one, he was startled to recognize someone. The soccer coach gave him a subtle fraternal nod as he stepped through the same automatic sliding glass doors Greg had just exited, but which hadn't closed yet behind him.

At the return end of the ferry he meant to go straight to his Jeep and head home, but instead he made a detour into the General Store. He wanted a prize for completing his errand on the mainland. He wanted a reward for not embarrassing himself by propositioning Mister Hot Soccer Coach. He wanted an Almond Joy.

They were out of Almond Joys. He bought a small bag of M&Ms instead. As his usual girlfriend at the register made change out of his twenty, he noticed plastic jars lined up on the counter. They had handwritten labels and little pink ribbons tied around their necks. The girl noticed when he picked one up.

"Disinfectant. Local product. We're out of Purell. The Swansons made up a batch in their bathtub. Don't know what's in it, but folks have been asking for it."

He put the bottle back, at the same time realizing he had no disinfectant at home. Formula 409, yes. Mr. Clean and Windex. But no disinfectant.

"Your change, Greg." She smiled when she used his name. "No live music this Saturday, by the way. That Mount Vernon band cancelled. Well, no, we cancelled them." Greg smiled back as he put his wallet back in his pocket.

"And it's too bad, I know, but we're going to do take-out meals starting tonight. Want to order something ahead of time?"

He said thanks anyway and walked out to the Jeep popping M&Ms into his mouth. Maybe he was a newcomer, and would be one for years, but he'd never be quite as new as anyone trying to come to his island this Saturday with a bass guitar.

The pork chop in the sink was defrosted by the time he got home. He was debating how to cook it when he heard a knock on his front door. A first.

A young boy, grasping the handles of his bike with mittened hands, stood under the light that illuminated the entrance to his house. He was wearing a Cub Scout shirt too big for him.

"Hello, mister. I'm Jeremy. Me and my mother live in the red house down the road." It wasn't that cold outside, but Jeremy was wearing a woolen ski mask that covered his entire face, as well as the mittens on his hands. Greg had no idea there was a red house down the road. It must be somewhere going away from the General Store and the dock, not toward them.

"I'm starting a business. I'm going to make deliveries for people. If you need anything from the store or somethin' to be picked up at the ferry, you can give me the money and I'll go get it for you."

Greg thought this was adorable. "Step inside out of the rain."

"I got my bike, mister. Plus I don't know you." Smart boy, he thought.

"How much do you charge, Jeremy?"

"For the delivery, one dollar each way."

Greg grinned. "What do you mean, 'each way'? Deliveries only go one way, don't they?" The boy was quiet for a moment. Perhaps he hadn't been asked this before. Perhaps his was the first house whose door he'd knocked on.

"Well, you might want me to get you somethin' at the store they don't got. So you would owe me one dollar. But if they *did* have it, and I brought it to you, then you'd pay me two."

"How old are you?"

"Nine."

"You'll make a million by fifteen." The kid blinked. Greg reached into his wallet and took out two singles. He thought: they don't make kids like this anymore.

"Mister, the store is closed now. I don't think I can get you anything."

"I know. This is an advance payment. You must have start-up expenses," he chuckled.

"Hey, mister, thanks!" Jeremy took the two dollars into one of his mittens and nearly dropped them when shoving them into a pocket.

"How do I contact you? When I want a delivery?"

"Oh, we have a phone at home. Do you have a phone, mister?"

"I do," he replied.

"Or you can tape a note to your mailbox down by the road. I'll check every day. Oh, cash only please. I don't have a bank account or anything."

"Cash it will be."

Before Jeremy mounted his bike to recruit the next house, he took the mitten off his right hand and extended his arm. Greg reached out automatically and shook it as it was offered. Only later, when sitting in front of his wood stove, did he think: the boy took off his mitten, the same mitten his mother probably told him to keep on at all times. *There's a virus out there.* Jeremy had taken it off because that's what one did. He recalled the precautions he had dispensed with over the years, too, as he welcomed embraces from men his own age just as naturally.

❖

Greg went to the G.S. on Thursday. He had an errand he couldn't delegate to a nine year-old. He was out of liquor.

The bottles of the homemade disinfectant on the counter were gone. In their place were smaller, brown ones, with printed labels. He picked one up as his girlfriend rang up his Wild Turkey.

"'Covid Cure-All'? What the fuck!" He apologized for his language and then continued. "Is this a joke?"

"Well, I don't know," she said through her facemask, sounding as if apologizing herself. "They were here when I came in this morning."

"There's no cure. You can't sell these!" Now he had made the poor woman uneasy, and he was sorry for it. He might be on this island for a very long time.

"So, someone's got a brother-in-law on the mainland who invented these. Someone must have brought a bunch over. Like I say, they were here when I got to work." More apologies all around this morning at the General Store. "They don't even have price tags on them yet."

"Sold any?" he asked, doing his best not to sound sarcastic.

"Two," she replied, as if that were good news. "Not sold, really. Gave. I told them they could pay later when I found out what they cost."

"Anyone sick on Guemes?" he asked. The girl shrugged. He asked that what he owed to be added to his account. On the drive back he wondered: What had his friends tried? Compound Q. Then that stuff you could only get in Japan. Saint John's Wort. He remembered the Saint John's Wort craze. It grew wild, cost-effective if worthless.

In the middle of the day he sipped his drink and listened on his laptop to the CBC relay of the BBC World News. The Chinese had built a hospital in ten days. Lombardy had declared a lockdown. Only a few cases elsewhere. Trump promised the number in America would soon go down to zero. Zero. Zero is a good number, a now lubricated Greg had to agree.

❖

Two days later and he hadn't left the house. It was perfect for him. He had much more space and light than he had in Seattle. It had a dishwasher, central air conditioning and a huge walk-in shower. It wasn't large large, a little tight for two people to live there all the time, unless they were lovers and not even then. He was all right alone, for the time being anyway. He lived by himself in Seattle after all, and it had become harder to find guys to do things with—some of his friends had cashed in on the real estate market and moved to houses in Palm Springs with swimming pools; others, renters, had been forced out of Seattle and were living in suburbs he needed his GPS to find. There was, of course, the chance he'd make new friends on Guemes. They didn't have to be gay; he was well beyond his child-bearing years. But how to make friends here was the issue. Become a volunteer fireman? Start going to church?

Another problem: no gym. He'd jog. He didn't have running shoes, but he did have a good pair of sneakers. That afternoon he donned a hoodie, a pair of shorts, and went out to the main road. Running felt good: the air was crisp, and unlike in Seattle no traffic lights to slow him. He didn't run very fast but he ran at a steady pace. He looked ahead to where the road stopped at the horizon: it couldn't go on forever, the island wasn't that big. No one ever knew what lay around the corner, but he decided decades ago to believe, despite all evidence to the contrary, life was long.

A pick-up truck eased out of a side road and turned his direction. It slowed down as it approached. He saw an old Obama sticker on its front fender, and he could tell who was driving. It was the Soccer Coach. Their eyes met. They nodded. He was certain now he had company on the island. They might never talk much less ever visit each other, but he knew and the Soccer Coach did as well. When the pick-up passed, he paused before turning his head to watch it disappear in the opposite direction. Out of breath, he turned and walked back to his house. He was looking down as he ambled up the driveway and didn't see the envelope taped to his front door until he was about to let himself in. He opened the envelope to find a dollar bill, four quarters and a sheet of lined paper folded into thirds.

The first paragraph was in a child's block letters.

Dear Neighbor. I'm Jessica, Jeremy's mom. I am writing this note to thank you for telling my son you'd help him out with his delivery business. But his grandmother and I have decided he is too young and, given the caranavirus, not the right time to help with our neighbors' errands. Thank you anyway! J

Below was another paragraph, written in an adult's cursive.

Neighbor! Jeremy says these two dollars (enclosed) belong to you—thanks for trusting him with it but as explained above, I guess we're all on our own until summer when they say the coronavirus will go away. See you around the island! Jessica.

He took off his sneakers, stripped, and threw his running clothes onto the floor. Beneath the showerhead he thought about both the little boy and the Soccer Coach. At least he knew the kid's first name. But he might never learn the Soccer Coach's, and he was overcome with a loneliness he hadn't felt since Steve died, a loneliness on a small island now made smaller by an invisible invader from the other side of the world. He'd come to Guemes for solitude, but what he got was loneliness. This is the loneliness, he mused under the assault of hot water, that everyone must dwell within their last moments, whether holding hands with a loving family or pinned to a hospital bed by a ventilator down your throat.

He was getting gas at the General Store when he heard the latest. If he didn't get his news via his laptop, he got it by eavesdropping.

Greg didn't know who Susan was, but now he learned she worried she had the virus.

"What are her symptoms?" one man asked the other.

"Dry cough, headache."

"Could be anything."

He had heard *could be anything* twice in his life. Once from a trick who called to warn him he might have something; and the other from Steve, by which time both men knew that anything was always something, when there were so many things. He might have heard it other times as well, when it was an all-purpose gay euphemism for time-to-say-goodbye-but-we-won't.

"Where'd she go?"

"Anacortes Island, I think."

"Good doctors there."

The two men ended their conversation in front of the pumps at the same time he got back in his Jeep, made a sharp turn, and got in line for the next ferry. He was making his first trip down to Seattle. The ferrywoman wasn't there to tell him to pull up closer to the car in front of him, so he didn't. He left more room than usual—a good six feet, in the spirit of the times. He turned off his engine and wound down his window. On the passenger seat next to him were four rubber bands and two folded handkerchiefs. Two different colors. He had to laugh. He had them there for going to the Safeway or the Bank of America. This was his first accommodation with the recommended facemask, but not the first time he'd used the handkerchiefs. He'd bought them for the bar long before there were viruses, now two of them, for him to worry about.

He thought about the woman at the hospital. What was her test like? Do they even have the test? He hadn't listened to the local news today, but yesterday they were out. He remembered his first test. The results took two weeks. They made him come back to the clinic to hear the verdict. We have a counselor in the next room, the nurse said to him, if you'd like to talk to someone. He didn't. He'd passed his test and didn't want to hear any more about it. Would there be someone to counsel Susan?

He unfastened his seat belt and got out of the Jeep. He strolled past the cars in front of him and went to the ferry ramp, below which the ocean was churning. I still can't swim, he said to himself. Just because his parents were afraid he'd catch polio at the Y. He looked across to Anacortes. If his life depended on it, he couldn't swim to it. He heard the sound of a squeaky bike behind him. He turned and saw Jeremy. He didn't have his ski mask or mittens on. Jeremy said hi mister and Greg said hello back. Jeremy rode his bicycle in tight circles on the asphalt road. We'll be boarding soon, he thought, and Jeremy will have to get out of the way. Each would wave to the other as Greg drove his Jeep onto the ferry deck for the long drive home.

A GUIDE TO WHATEVER THIS THING IS

Sam Nulman

After the website has approved your new photos, enter "tops" and "versatile tops" in the search bar like you do every day. Through sunken half-closed eyelids, scroll through the litany of men looking to penetrate a hole, any hole. Bored, click on profiles of boys whom you barely find attractive. Message them "hi" or "sup" or less subtle, "wanna fuk?" Vacantly fiddle with your perfunctory erection while you peruse, yawning at your computer screen. Roll your eyes at the noises of your roommate through the wall, laughing with the incessant morning happiness of a girl who has a boyfriend. Glare daggers at the wall as if she can somehow sense your frustration through the Sheetrock and as if you can stop her from being happy for the good of the apartment as a whole. Keep scrolling. Your phone buzzes, glance at it. Ignore the text from the boy that fucked you yesterday. It was okay but you don't feel he deserves a repeat performance. Feel slightly flattered, however, that he wants your ass again this soon.

You have a message on the website. Open it. It is from a semi-blurry seemingly semi-handsome man with the screen-name "bukketman." He asks what you're into. Reply "getting fucked in any and every position imaginable." Turn away for a moment and take a sip of water from your nightstand. Stare out the window and feel your body turning inward, like the implosion of a star. You feel a sneeze coming, let it come. It won't come. Fuck. You hate that. Now you really *are* depressed. Bukketman writes back. He says, "get over here right now" and beneath that, his address in the financial district. Remember that you are a hole, any hole.

Walk to the train and feel empty. Sit on the train and feel tired. Walk from the train to his building and feel nothing. Notice, as you enter the elevator and press the button for the 16th floor, that the building must have been designed for rich dickheads and that you are most likely about to get plowed by one. Walk through the cold modern metallic hallways to the door and knock. Sigh and fidget with your keys in your pocket. He answers the door, smiling, overly friendly, "Hi!" and invites you inside.

His teeth are large and white like a chipmunk's, his gums are long and his upper lip doesn't cover it up all the way. He is far more handsome than you expected, tall, lanky, chiseled jaw with five o'clock shadow. He radiates joviality and it forces a slight yet sincere smile out of you. Feel your numbness melt in his presence as you forget everything.

The apartment is bare, though nice. You only have a few seconds to look around because his tongue is already in your mouth and his hands are squeezing your ass. Kiss him back, hard. Put your hand on his hardening cock over his pants and rub. Allow him to undress you and toss you on the bed. His cock is pretty: suck it. He makes loud, appreciative moans and you like this. Put a condom on him. Notice his sexy and slim body while he fucks you on your back, harder and harder. Feel inadequate as you look down at your own body and can't help comparing. He announces he is about to cum. Command him to cum inside you. He does. His body convulses, he shouts in orgasm and you like this. Now you cum.

Laugh. Both of you laugh like, "ha ha can you believe we just did that goofy thing with our bodies?" He kisses you and you like this.

He flops down onto his back and says, "I'm very glad you came over."

"Me too."

Exchange names. Laugh about how this stranger just came inside you but you waited until afterwards to get each other's names. Roll your eyes (but on the inside where he can't see) at the fact that you've shared this post-fuck name exchange chuckle with many a man before him.

He asks, "Are you a student?"

Say yes and tell him about your major and try not to look too bored. Ask him, "What do you do?"

"I'm a chef. Well I'm going to be a chef. Right now I guess I'm more of a line cook."

Wonder how much money line cooks make but don't ask. Now make a joke, any joke. Show him you're funny and worthy. He laughs a real laugh. He jokes back, he's semi-funny too, though not as funny as you and you like this. You must always be the funny one. He just needs to laugh along and keep up. Talk about TV shows you like. His jaw drops as you tell him that you like that one show—*nobody* likes that one show. You tell him about more shows and movies you like and he can't believe that you both have the same taste, the same sense of humor, because like, what a rarity for two people to enjoy things that, up until now, felt specifically made for you alone. He tells you that he is here visiting for a specific job at a fancy restaurant before he goes back to culinary school in Napa Valley at the end of the year. Try not to look disappointed; you just met him.

Wait two days. You are at your friends' apartment while they play video games. Casually scroll through your phone and come across his number which he gave you before you left his place. Call him. Feel bold and different for doing this. You've never done this. He picks up with that convivial "Hi!" and you light up inside, a little. Cut to the chase.

"Hey, would you want to go on a date?"

"Yes I absolutely would!"

Make plans to go to that nice barbecue place down the street from you. Notice that his voice, now isolated from his body, sounds kinda valley-girl. Decide you don't care. You used to care but now you know better than to care about something as silly as a feminine voice. But then wonder, is it that his voice was girly or that it sounded like a specific kind of girl that you find unappealing? Don't think too much about how awful you're being. Hang up and rejoin your friends.

Spend a little more time on your outfit and ask your roommate what she thinks of it. She runs her fingers through your hair and gives you a thumbs up. You hear knocking. Check yourself in the mirror one last time. Answer the door. He is here to walk you to the restaurant even though it's only one block away. Your smile grows wider. You feel like a proper lady on a proper date even though you're both men and you've already exchanged fluids.

He's wearing a nice vertical striped button-down and his hair is hardened into porcupine spikes by too much gel. It reminds you of the guidos from back home that you hated. Order a drink because he ordered a drink. Order a side because he ordered an appetizer. Mimic his order for an entree, he's been here before and you haven't. Hope against hope that he pays for all of this. Tell more jokes. He laughs and his laugh is real. Make him like you. You can see that he likes you but really drive it home. Make yourself sparkle. Make your personality explode like a fucking H-bomb. Obliterate him. Brandish your comic ability like a poisonous blade and infect him with adoration. You are killing this. You can see in his eyes that you are killing this. Fuck, he's got gorgeous eyes. Even despite the terrible hairstyle, he's so very attractive to you. Handsome *and* laughs at your jokes? He may be perfect.

Offer to pay half the bill. Be slightly disappointed that he allows you to. He walks you back to your place and he says he wants to see you again. Tell him you'd like that. He kisses you. It feels bigger and better than the other day. He asks if he can come up. Hesitate but then realize y'all already fucked and you're not a proper lady and so let him upstairs.

Talk to him every day. Fuck like you're saving the world. Fuck like you're all out of time. Fuck because it's your favorite thing to do with him. One night, he invites you out to a club. He's been drinking with friends for a while already. Arrive, buy a drink, approach him, he tells you he is tired and going home. Breathe in to say something in confusion. He kisses your open, questioning mouth and takes his leave. Sip your drink and awkwardly stand near his friends attempting conversation. Disinterested, they dance away from you. Stay for ten more minutes and go home frustrated. A few days later, while cuddling on the couch, bring this up and tell him that it bothered you. Address it head on. He lets out a half-hearted "sorry." Don't let it go, try to explain. He puts his mouth over your mouth and stifles your complaints. Have sex on the couch. Let it go.

Go out one night to a bar, just the two of you. He tells you he talked to his mom about you. Tell him you told your sister about him. Say, "Yeah, I was talking to her and I said, 'this guy I'm dating is—'"

"Wait. Are we *dating*?"

"Um…I mean—"

He nods his head, contemplative. His eyes beam into yours. He states with certainty, "We're dating."

Your smile grows wider. Kiss him. You have a boyfriend now.

Go to lunch. A young boy holding a chart walks in asking for money for his school basketball team. Your boyfriend stares at the boy with disdain. Give the boy a dollar. Your boyfriend now stares at *you* with disdain. The boy leaves. With condescension in his voice, your boyfriend says, "That was nice of you."

He rolls his eyes and digs his fork into his french fries. Chew your food and ponder who it is you're dating.

Go out drinking and dancing more and more nights. No, it's not really your thing but it is *his* thing so just go out with him and pretend you love to dance. Stay until 3 am one night and as he goes to hail a cab home, kiss him sweetly and tell him you'll see him tomorrow night for dinner. A cab pulls up.

He says, "Okay. I love you."

Drop your jaw and stop your breath. He does the same.

Utter, "What?"

His eyes go wide, in either terror or a sneaky satisfaction, you can't tell which, and he says, "Nothing. Tomorrow—see you."

He leaps into the cab and it takes off. Stand on the sidewalk, frozen. Call your roommate and demand she come down to the bar at once. Tell her what happened. She asks if you love him. Say you don't know, well, oh fuck, you don't know. Say, well, yes, I guess, maybe? Fuck, you don't know. Pick up your phone in front of her and call him. You get his voicemail. Leave a message as you stare into the eyes of your roommate.

"Hey, um, well, shit, wow. You know what…fuck it! I love you too. I love you. Yeah. I think I love you. Fuck. Wow."

Hang up and slam your head down into your arms against the bar. Your roommate looks at you through suspicious eyes. Wonder if she's wondering if that was all performative.

In the morning, text him an apology. Say "we were both drunk haha."

He responds, "I love you. Just saying."

Your smile is so fucking wide it's trying to escape your face.

Stop using condoms. He says I love you as he cums inside you.

He shaves off his beard in your bathroom but leaves the mustache and walks in with a smirk. Your knees buckle, you tell him how he looks like a creepy perv and it makes your dick so hard it hurts and then he fucks you for the third time this morning. He shaves off the mustache now because he's got to go to work. As he tries to leave, grab him and make out with him. Get on your knees in the open doorway of your room and blow him as he laughingly gripes that he must go to work. He acquiesces. Swallow his cum. Kiss him. He leaves for work. You feel whole. You feel full. You feel everything.

At his apartment, try to decide on a movie. Flip through his DVD collection. You are baffled by his lame choices. He tells you not to judge him on this, and he swears he's not some vapid basic idiot. Think of him as a vapid basic idiot. Suppress this thought and remember that you are in love and that common likes and interests are a superficial type of connection anyway. Play a video game with him and his roommate. As he reaches a critical point in the game, tap his controller so that he fucks up. Laugh, it's a video game, and this is just for fun. He cocks his head, his mouth agape, and glares at you with true hatred. He tries to tear your skin from your bones with his eyes. He punches you. Keep laughing, sorta. He punches you again. Hard. And he punches again and again and you are not laughing and his roommate uncomfortably looks away. Try to block him. He punches you again and again, very hard. Fall over the side of the couch, bruised and confused. His roommate leaves. He goes to the bathroom for a long time. You lie on the floor, your body pulses, stunned.

Eventually, he comes back from the bathroom, apologetic. He admits he may have overreacted. Say nothing. He bends down to kiss you. Let him. You love him. Get up and walk to the bathroom. He follows you in there and pulls down your pants to fuck you up against the sink. Let him. You love him.

He finishes and takes you by the hand to the couch and spoons you. Cuddle for an hour. Feel warm, so warm, an interior heat you've never felt before. Pray this never ends. Your body pulses, stunned.

Lie in bed with strep throat on Thanksgiving. Don't think about him. You haven't heard from him in a week. It must just be the holidays. Don't think about it. He's busy. The last time you spoke, he gave you that dreamy look and told you he loved you. Don't worry. He's preoccupied with family. Shut up. Don't worry.

You've been sick for two weeks, and you've taken medication, but it won't go away. You receive a call from the pharmacy. There was a mix-up. The antibiotics they gave you were not antibiotics but steroids.

Mouth agape, baffled, bluntly declare, "This is malpractice."

The pharmacist says, "I understand."

His understanding does not eliminate your illness. Another week goes by with no word from boyfriend.

You knew it. You fucking knew it, you fucking idiot. Actually, stop it, don't do this. It can't be possible that someone can say "I love you" and then disappear with no warning. It's just not done. Pace around your apartment. Contemplate. Call him. Leave a voicemail.

"I guess you're still home for Thanksgiving? I guess we're breaking up? I don't know what to do here."

Try your best to cry. Scrunch your face up and try to squeeze the tears out of your constipated eyes. It doesn't happen. You can't get the sadness out. You feel it, it burns, but it won't come out. Pace. Listen to depressing music. Try to cry again and fail. He's just a boy. It just must not hurt that much. Remember that it is his birthday. It hurts so fucking much.

A day and a night pass. He calls. He doesn't address his absence no matter how hard you pry. He says you can meet up for dinner. He's allowing you to meet him for dinner. He's bringing his roommate. Baffled, force *your* roommate to come too. Meet at an Ihop. Get him a present. Maybe this isn't all over—get him that chocolate from that place he likes. Meet up outside the Ihop, the four of you, and awkwardly hand him the bag of chocolate. Your roommates introduce themselves to each other. Be somber. Let your bitterness show through your face and your silence. Take a booth.

While he and the roommates make small talk, stare at him as if your gaze can make him sorry. Wonder if a person can be made to feel sorry. Wonder if a person can fall out of love in an instant. The waiter brings waters.

Say, "You are a god amongst insects."

You've bizarrely quoted an X-Men movie to the waiter for no apparent reason and your maybe-boyfriend looks at you, incredulous, as if you farted those words out of your ass-mouth and he can't believe he let you touch his body.

After the meal, he quickly hops into a cab. His roommate, face contorted in apology, hugs you and says "goodbye" in a way that seems like she knows it's the last time you'll ever see each other. They speed away in the cab. Fume. Your roommate looks at you as you fume. Walk together for a block before she blurts out, "I'm so relieved."

Jerk your head in her direction, aghast. Let her continue.

"I always fucking hated that guy."

"Really?"

"He's like a vapid valley-girl douchebag. He sucks, man."

Don't know how to feel. Feel a bunch of things at once.

Whine about it. Go on and on and fucking on for three months. Play the role of the bitter ex-boyfriend. This is your identity now. Go to a bar with your roommate and whine like you always do. She explodes, "I'm so sick of hearing about this fucking guy! It's enough already, find something else to talk about."

Stare at her, stupefied, stunned into silence. Ponder if you're boring now.

Realize, holy shit, yes, you're boring now. Delete his number. Try to let him go. Your roommate tells you she is moving to California. You will need to find a new place to live in a few weeks.

Graduate from school with a bachelor's degree in fuck-all and zero prospects. Put all your belongings in storage and sleep on your sister's couch. Remind yourself and everyone else that this is only temporary. Your sister and her basic roommates ask you to tell them jokes and you oblige. They laugh. You are a novelty monkey on demand.

Create a dating profile out of boredom. Expect nothing. Talk to one cute boy for a while but never meet up. Text each other pleasantries and possible availabilities, but always have some excuse.

One day, alone and half-naked on your sister's couch, you receive a phone call from a number you don't know. Answer.

His valley-girl voice exclaims, like the first time you met, "Hi!"

Your stomach drops, your mouth is dry. It's been months with no sign of him. You wondered if, and hoped, he had died. You're not sure it's him. It can't be him.

Respond, "Hi, who is this?"

"…Ha. Oh. I guess you deleted my number. It's me."

Wonder if you have two stomachs because you feel it drop again and your mouth is immediately arid. He asks if he can see you tonight, 8pm, some finance bro bar in Murray Hill. Think "no" but say yes. Shower for the first time in a week. Dress with purpose. Realize for the first time, the only reason people try or care is to lure someone into loving them.

Arrive before he does, because of course. He walks in wearing a nice striped shirt. Be mad for some reason at the nice striped shirt. He smiles big and hugs you hard. He sits and bombards you with small talk. Napa was boring but the culinary school was an enriching experience, he thinks. He's been back in New York for three weeks, and is in a new apartment in Battery Park. He talks at you for five minutes without stopping, as if none of it happened, as if he didn't rip open your life with a serrated bayonet and take a shit inside your sense of reality. You can't take it anymore. Stop him mid-sentence.

"Okay. Small talk over. Are we gonna talk about it or...?"

"Ha. Um. I just thought we'd catch up—"

"Blah blah, bacon's still salty, you broke my fucking heart."

He nods. He admits it: he was a douche.

"I was talking with my mom and she told me I have a problem with avoidance. I realized I didn't want to be with you and I should have been honest with you but instead I disappeared. And you didn't deserve that. I'm so sorry."

Hear only parts of what he says. Hear only, "I didn't want to be with you."

He nervously chuckles and adds, bafflingly, "And when I said I love you, I was really drunk."

Do not respond to this, there is no response. Do not remind him that he said it a thousand times and he wrote it down and was he drunk the entire time? Hold this moment in your mind, now, and for years to come: the first man to tell you he loved you tried to take it back.

He tells you he wants to be friends. He says you're so funny and he wants you in his life. Tell him through a ruptured voice that you don't want to be his friend. Tell him he's a bad person. He shakes his head as if not computing.

"I'm a good person."

Shake your head as if not computing. He asks what it will take for you to be friends with him. He asks if maybe you just need to let out your anger? He looks at his watch and says, "It's 8:30. How about this. You have until 9 to say anything you want to me. Anything at all, just let it out. And then we can be friends."

Ask him if he's sure he wants to hear it. He smiles and nods. Release the kraken.

Spit your hate at his face. Wield your words. Your vitriol exits your mouth with a force beyond your control. Tear him from taint to teeth. Dress him down from every angle, his immaturity, his patterns of avoidance, he is vapid, he is vain, he is empty. Paint him like a clown fucking himself with a hand mirror. Explain the difference between a "good person" and a "bad person."

Look at your watch and say, "Oh. Nine o' clock. Shame. I wasn't done."

His mouth agape, face flushed, eyes a little wet, he clears his throat and says, "No one has ever said those things to me before."

Smile with anger and firmly state with meaning, "Good."

Remember this for years to come as the moment you should have gone home, redeemed. How cool it would have been if you had just said "good," shot up off the barstool and beelined home, pride intact. Try to blot out what happens next.

Stay and drink more. He buys beer flights and vodka shots. Betray yourself by accepting his further company. Get very drunk and forget why you were ever mad. He morphs back into the charming, handsome man with whom you have such chemistry. Laugh and joke and feel him inching closer in his chair, touching your arm, caressing your arm, groping your arm. Tell him through laughter that you hate him. He kisses you. Let him kiss you and hate yourself for it.

Make out in front of the bar. He tells you to come home with him.

Say, "Fuck you."

Make out some more. He tells you again to come home with him. Say, "Okay."

Make out in the cab. Make out in the lobby of his building. Make out in the elevator. Get in his bed and tell him that you're not going to have sex. He nods, knowing this isn't true. He puts on the movie "Airplane" and you both pretend you're going to watch it. Kiss violently. He unzips your pants. Zip them back up. He unzips them again. Leave them unzipped. Graze his erection over his underwear before gaspingly pulling your hand away like you just touched a hot stove. He grabs your hand and places it back on his dick. Rub. Kiss. Say, "I love you."

He winces, "Oh…I care about you so much…"

Push his body off of your body in disgust. Shiver with embarrassment. Turn over and tell him not to touch you. You have unlaced your ribcage, revealed your most vulnerable parts, and invited disease and disaster inside. Tell him you are too drunk to go home so you will sleep here but he is not to touch you.

Wake up, it is morning. Inexplicably try to kiss his closed mouth in some kind of foolhardy Hail Mary? He recoils and smiles in pity. Get dressed.

He asks, "So can we be friends now?"

Say nothing and leave.

Walk along the river and try to find a good spot to jump. Wander the city knowing this will be your last day on earth. You have no dignity, no pride, no prospects. You are a sad gay idiot. Soon you will be a dead gay idiot. Resent the fact that someone so dopey could push you to the margins of yourself. Resent the fact that the one who feels the least, wins. And how does that make any sense? Aren't feelings supposed to be the central point of life? If you feel nothing, you lose nothing and you gain nothing. You have lost yourself but he will remain in stasis. It's a bad video game. It's a joke without a punchline.

Your phone buzzes. It's an internet boy you've never met but whom you'd absently spoken with, on and off in the months since your now ex-boyfriend disappeared. He asks what you're up to. Tell him to meet you at The Blind Tiger in the West Village in an hour. A last ditch effort. If you're going to die, might as well fit in one last drink with a boy. He says yes.

Through sunken half-closed eyelids, glance at yourself in a reflective car window as you walk to the bar. You look like shit and you don't care. Roll your eyes at the people passing by holding hands and glare daggers at their interlaced fingers as if you could somehow rip them apart with your eyes. Adjust your gaze to stare past them and feel your body turning inward, like the implosion of a star. You feel a sneeze coming, let it come. It won't come. Fuck. You hate that. Now you really *are* suicidal.

Vacantly yawn as you enter the bar and find him ordering a drink.

He is a very tall and adorable boy in glasses and stylish clothing draped over his spindly skeletal frame. His face is winsome and boyishly British and his eyes are pools of calm blue. He is much cuter than you anticipated, and his aura of nervousness as he shakes your hand, somehow makes him more charming. He smiles the best and dorkiest smile and you notice he has adult braces which force a slight yet sincere smile out of you. Feel your numbness melt in his presence as you forget everything.

THE CAPTAIN

Morgan Hufstader

The mermaid was injured when Captain first set eyes on her.

They were dredging the remains of a wrecked ketch at the tip of Queen Anne's Teeth—the jagged rocks hidden under the shadow of the hills. Too many ships didn't see the teeth until it was too late, which made it the perfect place for the White Rose to lie in wait.

They cheered when her hull cracked. When she sank. Waited three days until the small figures bobbing in the waters stopped screaming, then stopped flailing, then stopped altogether.

Then the crew unknotted the rowboats, dropped them, and paddled swiftly towards the wreckage like water striders.

Captain stayed with the Rose. They were poring over the map, deciding on where best to deliver the bounty: the merchants at Hounds' Rock were owned by Cressida, and she'd given them a raw deal last time—the bitter bitch—but the sailors at New Harbor might trade with them if they cleaned up a bit, shined that silver tooth when they smiled—

"Cap'n, looks like they got a live one!" the lookout shouted from the deck.

A live one? Prisoners were only another mouth to feed, and they could barely keep fed the ones they had. Captain left the table and threw open the twin doors of the quarterdeck. Dry, salted wind blew knots of silver hair back, and Captain shoved it under their hat as they turned their gaze towards the rowboats bobbing steadily closer.

The first boats to cast on were piled high with as much as they could carry without taking water: goblets, blades, ropes, a brass lantern, a chest of garments, necklaces and rings, bracelets of gold and silver.

Anything that could be hocked, used, or consumed had been stripped from the wreckage.

Captain prowled the edge of the deck as the last boat approached the ship. It was helmed by Noam, the captain's first mate, a sturdy man with black hair and clever eyes, who should have known better than to bring a live thing on board. A figure was bundled up in blankets.

"Permission to board, Captain," Noam requested as he held to the side of the ship. His tone was measured, watching the captain's face with his deep-set eyes.

"Not until you tell me what the hell you're boarding with," the captain responded.

"I told him it was a bad idea, Captain!" squawked one of the crewmates suddenly. "It's bad luck!"

Noam lifted an oar and prodded the other's man's chest with the dripping end, so hard that it sent him splashing overboard. "The only bad luck is your yellow-belly, coward!" Noam spat.

"Enough!" Captain snarled, and Noam settled back in his spot, while someone helped the fallen man back aboard. "Lift the sheet."

Two men took the edges of the blanketing and tossed it back. When the captain saw what was underneath, a knot formed in their throat, as though they'd swallowed a pearl.

She was beautiful. Long, dark hair that flowed down her back. A voluptuous form made of waves. A face perfectly sculpted with gentle lines—a hint of eyebrows, a small nose, and plump, shell-pink lips. Her arms were bound with rope at the wrists and folded in front of her full, naked breasts.

Beautiful, but not human. At the wideness of her hips, her skin changed from ghostly white to blue-green, luminescent scales that shimmered when the light hit them. Her lower half was one long tail that fanned out at the end like a fish's.

Mermaid. The things that lead sailors to their doom.

But she seemed so incapable of hurting anyone. She was unconscious, injured—a purpled welt at the side of her head, a red slash across her side.

"Figured she'd go for a pretty coin," Noam said. "What with her being a live one and all."

"All the coin ain't worth our lives," the wet crewmember sniffled and Noam shot him a scathing look.

Noam was greedy, but he wasn't wrong. A mermaid caught live was a rare thing indeed. A couple seasons back, they'd found a kelpie swept up on shore. The thing'd been dead some time, its mane matted with sand, eyes plucked out by the savaging gulls, but they'd lugged the heavy carcass on boat, scrubbed the bones, and sold it to an alchemist at Crystal Cove's port market. That catch alone had been enough to keep the White Rose healthily stocked and sailing nearly a full season. And that one had been *dead*.

This creature was alive, her ribs expanding and compressing with each shallow breath.

"What d'you want us to do with her, Captain?" Noam asked.

Their little boat bobbed in the water beside the ship, waiting their captain's orders.

"Put her in the livewell," Captain said, and they hoisted the mermaid up and took her on board.

❖

They'd been at sea for 186 nights and days.

It grew tedious at parts. The crew, at least, had ways of entertaining themselves: they drank, played dice, and napped in the sun.

Captain didn't join their games. It was important to keep a divide between the crew and Captain. The closest Captain got to their crew was on the nights that they pulled the youngest crewman—Cromwell, the cherry-faced deck boy—into their quarters. There, the captain stuck their fingers inside of him until he squirmed and moaned and left wet, crusty stains on Captain's sheets.

They felt no affection for the boy, no attraction, even; rather, they liked the repetitive chain of events—touch produced pleasure and pain in an ebb and flow that could be replicated over and over with the same result.

Predictability was sacred.

Red sky at night meant glass-eyed sea in the morning.

A dead gull was always an omen of bad weather to come.

If it was Rihlan's turn to cook, half the crew would be sick the next day.

The captain relied on the things they could, because it was the things they couldn't—the unpredictability of the sea and the wrath of her temper—that got entire crews killed. The mermaid was an unaccounted element. The kind of disturbance that had a rippling effect and threw everything at a tilt.

Noam and a couple other mates stored her in the livewell—a pool that'd be carved into the floor below deck by the bilge, no more than four feet side and six deep. Meant to store live bait and fresh catches. The ship medic—a thick-chested man who amputated hands and feet without flinching—went down next. When he came back up deck he was sweating, pale, and stammered over his report. "Mild head wound, sutured the gash around her ribs, but there is—b-behind her ears, I mean—it's ah—well—oddities…"

Then he went down deck, mumbling, blotting the back of his neck with a handkerchief.

They anchored the White Rose there a couple days more, picking at the bones of the sunken ship until there was nothing left, and then separated and divvied up the riches. The captain set a new course for Crystal Cove, thinking that the alchemist and his bones might know what to do with their latest catch.

At this rate, there was a good chance the mermaid wouldn't live through the trip, anyhow. She'd woken, but she'd been wilting—she wouldn't eat what food the crew threw at her, wouldn't respond to them, and when Captain looked in on her, they could see the human-half of her crooked against the round opening of the well. She leaned awkwardly on her bound arms, head flopped to the side. When the ship rocked and the sun from the port windows swept slowly over the tank, Captain could see that her scales looked like they were molting, their shimmer now milky and dulled.

❖

The captain had had terrible dreams. Recurring dreams. Dreams of sinking, of a wall of blue swallowing them down.

They reach upwards to claw through the water. Their lungs feel tight and ready to burst.

Then, suddenly, they can breathe. And they let the ocean take them.

❖

When the captain woke this time, their quarters smelled like sour milk and body sweat. Lingering hints of Cromwell.

Aching for fresh air, Captain donned a tunic and trousers, tying the whole thing off with a belt. They exited the quarterdeck and felt relief at the brush of cool air that hit them. The stars were out, the moon a sliver, and Captain could see a lantern winking on the main deck, where the night shift kept an eye on the seas.

To get to the bilge, the captain had to go downstairs, through the gallery, past the horde of men snoring in their bunks, until they reached the door. They left their own lantern, knowing the ship well enough in the dark.

Inside, there was a strange sound—a clicking—repetitive, rapid, and the rustling of fabric.

Captain stepped closer to the well, towards the sound. They could see the mermaid in the same spot she always seemed to be in: slouched half out of the water, bound arms to the side. A naked breast was exposed, the nipple hard and pink in the moonlight.

A low groan drew the captain to the culprit. A crew member was hunched a couple paces from the well, his hand down his trousers. His belt buckle made a clicking sound every time it was disturbed. He was staring straight at the mermaid, his mouth hung dumbly open, and he didn't seem to notice the captain until they removed their blade from the scabbard at their belt: "Put it away or I'll slice it clean from your body."

The crew member froze, then jumped to his feet and immediately began redressing with shaking hands and stammered apologies. He rushed out of the room, passed the captain, and closed the door behind him.

Now, they were alone.

There was nothing but the low creek of the ship's wood and the slosh of water from the well as the White Rose stayed back and forth. Captain stepped close to the mermaid, and she didn't budge—was she dead? Shrimp and minnow in the live tank crawled and picked at the mermaid's scaly tail. Moonlight fell in through the oval port window, and the captain crouched down at the edge of the well and took the mermaid's chin in their hand, turning the thing to face them.

"Well?" Captain said. "Just you and me now. Are you alive then? Can you speak?"

No words. She just stared, her eyes too big, and blinked, a rapid shutter of green and white.

Alive, at least.

Captain reached again for the dagger. When they withdrew the blade, the mermaid's eyes caught the shimmer. It moved—a sudden jerk away—and small flaps behind her ears suddenly flew forward, like tiny blue-green fans. The mermaid's lips parted and she let out a noise—a hiss. A warning.

The captain held up a palm. "Settle down," they said and then pointed to the mermaid's hands, bound in permanent prayer. "You'd like those gone, wouldn't you?"

The fins behind the mermaid's ears waved unsurely, then slowly relaxed back against the sides of her skull. Captain slowly took the mermaid's hands and pulled her forward. They pressed the blade to the ropes and gently sawed through one of the binds. Once it popped free, they sheathed the dagger and unwrapped the rest. The mermaid's skin was marked with indentations from the ropes, bruised purple and red in places.

The mermaid flexed and closed her fingers, which moved strangely from disuse.

"There," Captain said. "Better, isn't it?"

The mermaid reached forward suddenly, too quickly for the captain to pull away. Her fingers entwined with the captain's. They were soft where they should have been water-wrinkled—instead, they felt like the smooth belly of a conch shell. Captain's hands and arms, in contrast, were roped with sinewy veins and leathered from the torturous sun. They found themselves unable to move as the mermaid slowly scissored her fingers through theirs, the tips tracing the back of the captain's hands.

The touch created a sudden tightness in their chest. A blood-fever swam up their throat, making them choke on their words.

The mermaid didn't seem to mind. She just looked at the captain. Wide, gentle eyes.

"I won't let them hurt you," Captain said once their words returned to them. "I won't let anyone hurt you again."

❖

Captain took the ring of keys from their belt and locked the door to the bilge when they left. No one went in and out after that, no one except Captain, who had the master key.

They began visiting her more and more. The mermaid was eating again—the next time Captain went back, the mermaid had devoured everything in the live tank. They began bringing fish from the kitchen, which the mermaid would devour greedily. But she seemed to prefer, the captain thought, the fresh fish, still alive, which she could hunt in rapid circles around the well.

After a small game of chase, catch, and eat, which the captain watched from the side, trouser legs rolled up, feet dangling in the well, the mermaid lifted herself from the tank and wiggled between the captain's knees. Her hands slipped suddenly under the captain's tunic, wet paws sliding up Captain's skin and over their small breasts.

The mermaid dropped her forehead against Captain's and Captain could feel her warm breath—short and rapid—against their dry lips.

They made frequent trips at night and would leave each time with their tunic streaked wet from slippery hands.

When they left one evening, Noam was awake in the gallery. He was at the table, mending a fraying rope by wrapping the end of it and melting the tip in the open lantern. His thin eyes narrowed at the captain's approach.

"Been spending a lot of time with that thing, Captain," Noam said. "Hope you won't have trouble parting with it when we get to Crystal Cove."

The captain said nothing, just left Noam without another word.

❖

Behind the ear, at the place where the mermaid's skull curved into her neck, that's where the captain's exploratory fingers found her most vulnerable part. The skin turned blue, scaly, parted in a seashell shaped fin. If they traced their finger underneath the fin and peeled the cartilage back, there were the long slits. Gills. They remained dormant above water, but underneath, they expanded and contracted, pulling oxygen from the water.

The mermaid didn't let the captain touch her gills without squirming, but if they gently stroked the protective layer on top, the mermaid would rest her head in the captain's lap and close her eyes, cat-like, warm and trusting.

❖

Captain fell to the floor, panting.

Their body felt squid-like and boneless as it hummed and pulsed. Their head resting on the floorboards by the well, they heard the light splash of water, felt the mermaid's wet fingers withdraw from the place between their legs and run through the captain's hair instead. The touch was gentle, and the mermaid's nails felt good on the captain's scalp. The captain's eyes fell closed.

The hand retracted and water slapped against the sides as the mermaid arched up—Captain could hear the heaviness of her forearms knocking against the floor like little knees. Captain kept their eyes closed, even as they felt the nuzzle of the mermaid's nose on their cheek, the velvet soft pair of lips at that small stretch of skin under their ear.

And then a whisper. A throaty language.

The captain couldn't make out the words until later, until they'd left and returned to their own quarters. Until they'd taken a nip of whiskey, stripped out of their clothes, and dug into the warmth of their own bed.

Until they woke up that same night, the brightness of the moon spilling pale on their bed, all while the captain gasped for breath, heart hammering in their chest, because the mermaid's words had crystalized glass-sharp in their mind:

Kill them, she'd whispered, *kill them all and we can be together forever*.

❖

They were nearly to Crystal Cove when the storm hit.

Captain had kept an eye on the sky. It had been brewing slowly—grey, heavy clouds, the taste of metal in the air. They had half a day's stretch until they were within the safe arms of the cove, and Captain ordered their crew to tighten the mainsail and draw out the jib. But no matter how much speed they picked up, the weather caught up with them all the same.

When the swells rose, they battened down the hatches and rolled up the jib. They barely got the sheets tightened before the first drops of rain began to splatter on the deck.

Drops quickly turned to a downpour. Lightning lashed the sky and the waves churned the large schooner as though it were a child's toy. Crewmen shouted at each other over cracks of thunder and the captain's hair and clothes stuck to their body, heavy with rainwater. They blinked droplets from their eyes as they yanked the wheel back and forth, feeling the rudder protest and pull underneath their grip.

Impossible to see anything ahead of them. Or on either side. Lanterns rocked wildly and every now and then, someone blared the horn to alert passing ships.

Noam rushed up the steps to stand on the deck beside the captain, gripping the rail as a gust of storm-wind yawned the ship to the right. "Storm is drifting her too far starboard, Captain!" he shouted. "Nothing but rocks that way! Cove is twenty degrees that way!"

Noam pointed port-side and the captain felt the soreness in their jaw where their molars clenched. "I know these seas. Keep an eye out for other ships."

"Aye!"

There was worry in Noam's face. Nothing to do about that now, though.

They knew these seas.

They knew the entrance to the Cove—a channel wide enough to sail straight through.

They knew the cliffs to the right—the sea bottom filled with jagged rocks and teeth.

They knew how easy it would be for even an experienced captain to get pulled into the rocks.

It'd happened plenty of times before. No one would guess.

"Dead ahead!" screamed the lookout. "Brace for impact!"

But it was too late. The ship gave a shuddering groan as the hull ripped over the shallows underneath. Shouts from the crew. Roared demands. And then eyes on the captain. What do we do? What do we do?

We sink.

It took the ship a long time to fully submerge. Some men got into row boats that weren't guaranteed to shore. Others jumped. Captain stayed with the ship. The splintering wood let out roaring, dying-animal noises. The water gurgled up around the captain's boots.

Let the ocean take it, the captain thought. Let the ocean take it all.

The water was cold, the wind ripped and wailed, and the captain choked on the salty taste. The massive ship pulled the water around it into a cyclone, sucking up debris and planks and the screams of men who hadn't made it out in time. Captain took one rasping gulp of air and then was pulled underneath—

Quiet here. The turbulent waters twisted and tossed the captain around, spinning them until they couldn't see which side was up. Their arms flailed, catching nothing, and human panic seized.

She won't come for you. This was all for nothing. You'll die alone.

Raking at the water, kicking, fighting for air. Nostrils burned, eyes stung, lungs ached.

Until they felt it. Her small fingers lacing with their own.

She pulled the captain through the water so they were face to face, her wild hair dancing in the sea like a halo around her. The captain stopped reaching for the surface and reached for her instead, her small shoulders, her soft face. The pain subsided when Captain felt the gentle press of her lips against their own, lips cold as a corpse.

Captain took her hand. The mermaid pulled them down, her tail flowing behind her—she was strong here. At home.

And so was the captain.

The captain felt their legs twist and braid until the flesh bound into a single, flexible tail. Deeper the mermaid dragged them, and deeper the captain went, until they felt their lungs ready to burst. And when they released their instincts and opened their mouth, drinking the ocean in, they felt it happen; the skin under their ears broke into open slits.

And finally, Captain could breathe.

My Darling Socialist

Aaron Hamburger

I moved up to the University of Michigan in the fall of 1991, the day before the formal dissolution of the Soviet Union. My father was so excited (about Communism ending, not my college career beginning) that during our forty-minute car ride to campus, he kept fiddling with the AM Radio, searching for the latest news bulletins. Mom periodically reminded him to keep his eyes on the road while I stared resentfully out the window at the edges of leaves changing colors from summer green to autumn ruby, orange, and gold.

When we turned off the highway to approach Ann Arbor, Mom switched off the radio so she and my father could give me advice. They warned me to be careful about who I socialized with, and to resist the temptation to follow the latest intellectual fads, politically correct nonsense like "Adam and Steve" instead of "Adam and Eve," using the title "Ms." with women's surnames, or referring to Blacks as "African-Americans." As a final reminder to stay true to my ideals, they gave me a going-to-college present: a copy of the play *A Man for All Seasons*.

In my dorm room, Mom kissed my cheek and then searched my face. "I'm sure I'm forgetting to tell you something," she said, "but I can't remember what."

Dad lightly patted the side of my arm and said, "Keep your nose out of the bars."

Then they left me to unpack.

For a short while, I sat on the bed and surveyed all my stuff, crammed into plastic crates, duffel bags, and boxes. Finally, I thought, fuck it, and went out to look at men.

At my small suburban high school, staring longer than strictly necessary at a guy could get you beaten up. Plus, our class had just over a hundred kids total, meaning there weren't too many guys to look at, even if I'd been brave enough to look at them.

But in Ann Arbor, among a student body of thousands, I had my choice of men to look at, and they were all handsome. Or even if they weren't handsome, they were handsome by virtue of their being there. I loved the texture of their hair, whether curly, wavy, or smooth. I loved their bright eyes and curled lashes, and the sharp contours of their noses and their jaws, milky and clean-shaven, or deeply tanned with a light sheen like polished wood, or dusky and speckled with facial hair. I loved their rough capable fingers and oddly delicate ears. I loved the smooth planes of their chests and the curves of their hips and butts. I loved their meaty legs and surprisingly slim, even dainty feet. And their voices, those deep, craggy voices that echoed down dormitory halls or through the trees.

In the library, I'd look over the cover of the book I was holding and stare at men. In class, as the other students took notes or doodled in notebooks, I stared at men. I stared at them in the dorm, the cafeteria, while walking across the quad, wherever I went. Stare, stare, stare.

I didn't know what I wanted to do with men other than look at them, though I knew there were words for guys who liked to look at guys. I'd heard my father use those words to describe the effeminate owner of the boy's clothing store where Mom used to buy my gear for summer camp—even though the guy was married with children. What I didn't know was if those words applied to me. Or more truthfully, I did know, but I didn't want to know.

❖

One of the few men in Ann Arbor that I didn't enjoy looking at was the charismatic professor who taught my Intro to American History lecture, Mondays and Wednesdays from 9 to 10:30. From his perch at the front of the auditorium, he dropped f-bombs and referred to President Bush as Shrub and the Democrats competing to run against him next year as "the seven dwarfs." He referred to the Middle East as: "a region with which you may be familiar, as we recently had occasion to bomb there."

Though he was brilliant and entertaining, he was not pretty, with a mass of tangled dark curls and a bulbous red nose. Once after class, when I went to ask him a question, I discovered that up close his cheeks were pitted and he was slightly cross-eyed. Also he wore sandals with white socks, a thing I had never imagined possible. Nevertheless, there was always a group of young women crowded around him, giggling and twirling their hair.

The TA who'd been assigned to lead my discussion section on Tuesday afternoons was more boring to listen to, but far nicer to look at. His name was Richard. Not Rick or Rich or even Dick. Richard. He was a tall handsome blond man with broad shoulders and a pale face whose blank expression invited me to study it further, to guess at his thoughts. Whenever our section met, Richard wore the same outfit: jeans and a white button-down shirt. They might have been the same jeans and shirt, unless he had a closet full of old jeans and white shirts. Either way, his clothes always looked worn and too tight, hugging the lines of his legs and butt. The buttons of his shirt strained to stay closed across his chest, and I kept wishing for them to pop open.

When I first got to college, I wasn't entirely sure what a TA was and why one person might be a TA and another might be a professor, or the difference between a 300-person lecture and a twenty-person discussion session. But I did learn quickly enough that though I'd rather stare at our TA, I'd much rather be taught by our professor.

Poor Richard would stand in front of our classroom, lean against the chalk railing of the blackboard, his pretty face and muscular poem of a body barely moving a muscle as he droned on in a whispery voice about labor movements, the social contract, or the Annales school of historians. He'd ask pointless open-ended questions, like "How does the message of the Wobblies resonate with you today?" "Do you see how despite the prevailing rhetoric of equality, American has always been ruled by a powerful oligarchy that reinforces prevailing social structures?" Usually I was the only one who answered, out of pity, or maybe so Richard would notice me: "The Wobblies were like labor unions today." "Is that like corporate lobbies donating to politicians to advance their agendas?" And once I said, "Nice shirt!"—this on the day he wore a pale blue shirt instead of his usual white. Richard blushed and said thanks.

During those pregnant pauses, while Richard waited for someone, anyone—well, for me—to speak up, sometimes I'd prolong the silence, just a bit, so I could draw him in my notebook. Richard had a noble profile like the image of Sir Thomas More on the cover of *A Man for All Seasons*, and I imagined he was a lionhearted prince or something, with an ancestral castle in England where we could live together and I could look at him to my heart's content.

❖

One of my tricks for looking at men was flyers.

Flyers were how you found out about everything, and they were almost as omnipresent as handsome men. Flyers were posted on kiosks and bulletin boards, left in messy stacks in dormitory common rooms, or taped to the ground in the shape of a giant M. They were also handed out by people standing outside classroom buildings, or in the "Diag," the central crossroads on campus. If those people happened to be male, then I'd stop and fumble with their flyers a bit, as an excuse to linger and look longer. I didn't care whether these men were promoting intramural water polo, a cappella choir, or Christian prayer fellowship circle. Futile and one-sided lust was my only religion.

One afternoon, while coming out of history class, I was offered an orange flyer by a man who asked: "Are you interested in independent voices and journalism?"

The man stood by a folding table with a stack of newspapers and a stack of flyers. He wore a blue and white pinstripe button-down shirt, pressed khakis, and penny loafers with actual bright and shiny pennies in them and no socks. His dark blond hair was combed in such a way so that each strand ran in the same direction and was cemented in place with gel. He looked less like a student than a model from one of those J.Crew catalogues that I hoarded in my desk like porno magazines. For me, the catalogues served the same purpose as porn, and it was safer to be caught with a drawer full of J.Crew than pictures of naked men.

He handed me a flyer, which I managed to drop on the floor, giving me an extra moment to stare at his sculpted chin. "Oops," I said. "Sorry about that."

As I kneeled to get it, he kneeled with me, and for a few precious seconds, we were huddled together on the ground, our foreheads barely a foot apart. Grabbing the flyer before I could, he handed it to me with a confident sweep of his arm and pressed his lips into a tight smile, as if it might be too feminine for a man to appear too cheerful next to another man. As we both rose, he said, "Do you read the *American Independent*?"

I looked at the flyer, which was promoting a mass meeting for new members interested in "a scholarly journal and bi-weekly forum covering campus affairs at the University of Michigan, free of liberal media bias."

"We believe in intellectual freedom," he said.

"Freedom sounds good." I glanced at the place where his buttoned shirt stopped being buttoned. A faint wisp of chest hair stuck out there. I bet his chest was the lightly hairy kind.

He handed me a newspaper to go with the flyer. "Come check us out," he said and stopped looking at me so he could offer his flyers to other students. It almost felt like a rejection, except that of course, by turning away, he gave me the chance to look at him more.

❖

Before returning to my dorm room, I ate dinner alone, as usual, in the cafeteria, the one place I didn't like to stare at guys. I felt too embarrassed, always on my own. A few tables over, I spotted my roommate, sitting with a friend and arguing loudly about Fortran.

I finished my dinner quickly, then deposited my tray in the kitchen and retreated up to my room. As I shut the door behind myself, I let out a long, deep breath.

In high school, I hadn't made many friends, much to the disappointment of my parents who'd worked hard to get me into a prep school so I could make connections that I could profit from later in life. My loneliness was in fact a survival strategy. Nervous that the other students might guess my secret, I kept my classmates at a distance. I learned to shape-shift and deflect attention, and in general to avoid having a fixed point of view on anything. If I wasn't a star, at least I'd kept my nose clean.

But now that I was in college, I was hoping to dirty my nose.

Before school began, we'd had the option of requesting a single or shared dorm room. I asked to share, imagining I might be assigned a hunky roommate whom I might occasionally glimpse naked. My roommate turned out to be a tubby engineering major with acne who was rarely around, always off in the computer lab or something. On the rare occasions when he ran in to change his clothes, he wrapped a beach towel around his waist before dropping his pants.

The other guys on my hall were far less modest, parading back and forth from the bathrooms in only their boxer shorts. I'd see them in their dorm rooms with the doors open, lying back on bean bag chairs with their legs spread wide and blasting songs like "Under the Bridge" by the Red Hot Chili Peppers, who famously performed onstage nearly naked, just with a sock covering their junk. Another popular song that fall was Jesus Jones's "Right Here, Right Now," celebrating the end of history, now that Communism was over.

Leaning against the door to my dorm room, I wondered what I'd do with myself until it was time to go to sleep. I had some reading homework for history class, which usually I made a point of doing, no matter how dry; otherwise, who would answer poor Richard's questions? But tonight, I couldn't concentrate on Oregon Fever or mass migration Westward. I felt too queasy and restless, too frustrated, and too angry about being alive.

I threw my backpack on the bed, and the rolled-up copy of the *American Independent* fell out of a side pocket. Flopping down on my bed, I grabbed the paper and began to read.

The front page featured headlines like "Date Rape: Fact or Myth?" and "Why Radical Left Professors Hate the Canon," a feature about a Great Books class that added to its curriculum a feminist revisionist novel about Cassandra by a writer from East Germany—yes, Communist East Germany of all places—for "balance."

Then I noticed an article below the fold, by a reporter who'd gone "undercover" to visit Lost Society, Ann Arbor's only gay bar. There was a gay bar in Ann Arbor? Certainly, no one was handing out flyers about it.

During the reporter's visit, Lost Society had only a few customers milling around, looking pathetic and lonely. The peppy dance music playing overhead sounded tragic floating over the empty dance floor. A stranger approached the reporter, offering to buy him a drink. This guy, who seemed pretty old in the reporter's opinion, maybe thirty or thirty-five, told a sob story about a string of failed romances. Toward the end of the story, the guy slipped a hand onto the reporter's left thigh. Indignant and alarmed, the reporter removed said hand from said thigh, jumped off his stool, and went home, slightly drunk and glad to be straight.

I set down the newspaper, my fingers smudged with ink. What would my parents say if they could see me now, reading about a gay bar? Whenever they called to check in on me, about once a week, they asked about my "social life," by which they meant girls. I said no in as surly a voice as possible to discourage further prying.

Usually I ended my evenings by opening *A Man for All Seasons*, a convenient hiding place for the men's underwear ads I cut out of the Sunday newspaper circulars, magazines, and a few of my J. Crew catalogues. Tonight, however, I didn't need the pictures. I kept thinking about that strange man touching the reporter on the thigh.

I was tired of looking. I wanted to touch.

Where was Lost Society? The article didn't give an address, just a general area. If there was an Ann Arbor phone book in our dorm, I'd never seen it, and I felt nervous calling information to ask for the number. So the next day, I left my room early on the way to class to wander the streets of downtown Ann Arbor, hoping I might bump into the bar.

I wandered for almost an hour, freezing in my T-shirt. Stupidly, I'd failed to register the change of seasons and didn't think to put on a jacket. I finally gave up the search and cut across the quad to get to Statistics 101, which I was taking to fulfill a math requirement. On the way, I noticed a stoop-shouldered tall man in a blue windbreaker handing out tiny red flyers, the size of a playing card. As I got closer, I realized the man was my TA Richard, and that he was surrounded by a small mob of guys who were jeering at him because he was there to promote the Young Communists.

Communism? Isn't that like dead, dude?

Communism? Why don't you move to Russia?

Though Richard was a head taller than his tormentors, he looked anxious and small, his face paler than usual, his bottom lip in a nervous pout, his shoulders slouched. One guy started imitating Richard in a Russian accent. Another grabbed his flyers and threw them in the air. As they came fluttering down, I wanted to rush to Richard's side to defend him, but I hung back, fearing I'd be branded a Communist, or worse.

Finally, the guys got bored of their teasing and moved on. Richard picked up the flyers that were scattered everywhere. I hesitated before going up to him—a real, live Communist collecting blood red flyers about Communism—but he was so damned cute.

I walked over and asked, "Are you okay?" What a stupid question.

"Yeah, I'm fine," he said in a flat voice, frowning at the ground.

"Do you need some help?" A lame question, since he'd already gathered all the flyers and was shuffling them into a neat pile. Richard handed me a flyer, and I shrank a bit, seeing the sickle and hammer. "Oh, thanks," I said. "So…how's business?" Was that the wrong thing to say to a Communist? I'd messed up again.

Richard shrugged. "Starting some conversations."

I couldn't picture Richard in conversation. For a socialist, he wasn't much of a socializer.

"Conversations about Communism," I said. What was the exact color of his eyes? Slate blue or cornflower blue? "Maybe you could have a conversation with me about it. I mean, look at the news, right? Hasn't it been proven that Communism didn't work?"

"A person doesn't depart from his ideals every time the wind changes. And if you're referring to the former Soviet Union, that wasn't true Communism."

"No?" This would be news to my father.

"No." Far more animated than I'd ever seen him, Richard began explaining about Marx and Engels, Communism versus Socialism, the idea of Marxist-Leninism as a transition phase to get to the end goal of Communism. I enjoyed listening to him, though I wished he'd move on from his political blah-blah-blah and divulge some personal tidbit about himself. An opportunity came up when he described the housing conditions in the slums of South Ann Arbor.

"Is that where you live?" I blurted out.

"No," he said, taken aback. "I'm in graduate housing."

"Do you live alone?"

"I have a roommate."

"Really?" I said. "I didn't picture you as having a roommate."

"Well, I do."

Maybe that was risky of me, admitting that I'd pictured his living situation as anything at all. Surely a presumed heterosexual wouldn't be picturing his TA outside of class. It was like that time in high school when I'd slipped up, drawing undue notice by complimenting a male teacher for his tie because it brought out the soft green of his eyes.

"I'm not keeping you, am I?" I asked. "From talking to people."

"Oh, that's okay. Not many people want to talk to me."

God, I loved his nose. Such a masculine, handsome, ramrod straight nose.

I was feeling bold that afternoon, so I said, "I don't mind. I like talking to you."

Richard coughed. "Well, I like talking to you too."

"Tell me more about where you live," I said. "What's it like, graduate housing?"

Richard looked confused. "Well, it's pretty much like any other kind of housing, I guess."

Maybe you'll invite me over to see it, I thought. Say it, say it. But I just watched him with a dopey look on my face.

I was late to statistics.

❖

The *American Independent* mass meeting was held in a basement meeting room at the Student Union, where John F. Kennedy had famously announced his proposal for the Peace Corps. At the door, I was given a nametag to stick to my shirt, and then I strolled into the room, wondering how I might find the reporter who'd written that article about Lost Society. Maybe I could ask him where exactly on his thigh the stranger had placed his hand.

I'd never seen so many blond people in one place. One of these was the guy who'd handed me the flyer inviting me here. He wore a navy blue blazer with khakis and he was surrounded by a small mob of guys in similar blazers and young women in pleated skirts.

Since coming to college, I'd grown used to milling around alone in spaces crowded with people who already knew each other. But within a minute of walking in, I was approached by several *Independent* staffers, saying, "Great to see you!" as if they'd been awaiting my arrival, though I guessed they were trained to say that to anyone with a "New Member" nametag.

One staffer, who had a thick mane of curly blond hair and big white teeth, shook my hand and told me she was the Managing Editor. "Did you meet Jeff yet?" she asked, then explained she meant the guy who'd given me the flyer. Jeff, so that was his name.

"Yes, I did," I said. "Jeff invited me to this meeting. Jeff's cool." It felt thrilling to refer to this Jeff by name. Out loud. I could repeat it to my parents when they asked if I'd met anyone. "Oh, yeah," I'd say. "I met Jeff."

"Everyone loves Jeff. Jeff's great. And he's a hell of a softball player too. We kicked the crap out of the *Michigan Daily* last year. But then, liberals are terrible at sports."

"I thought the *Daily* was just the college newspaper. I didn't realize it was liberal."

"Liberal as the day is long," she said. "Ooh, shh now. Jeff's about to speak."

Jeff climbed up onto a chair to welcome us all, and the blond heads fell silent and nodded to his words. After making a Mike Dukakis joke, he announced the *Independent* was having a Halloween bake sale next week. "We need everyone to sign up for a shift. And no stealing free cupcakes or cookies while you're on duty. We're for capitalism, folks, not welfare."

When he finished his speech, the managing editor jabbed me with her elbow, which hurt, and said, "Go say hi to Jeff!"

I edged closer to the circle of handsome well-groomed guys around Jeff and tried to catch his eye. Finally, I blurted out, "Hey, Jeff!" He and his friends gave me strange looks as if I'd invited them to join Richard's young Communist group. Why would I, a stranger, be talking to Jeff? *The* Jeff, who was "great." Jeff the Great. "I just wanted you to know," I said after a painful silence, "that I can help out with the bake sale."

"Excellent news, buddy," he said, patting my back. "Sign-up sheet's in the back."

"Oh, yeah," I said. "Of course. I'll head over there now."

As I walked away, the talking started up again.

❖

On my way into history lecture, a slender-looking guy with blond hair that fell over his right eye handed me a flyer. "Thanks for wearing blue jeans today," he said.

"Blue jeans?" I said.

"Today is blue jeans day. You're supposed to wear blue jeans if you support gay rights."

I looked at his outfit: a black turtleneck and crisp dark blue jeans. "I didn't know," I said, my voice cracking. "But everyone wears blue jeans."

"That's the point," said the guy. "Are you gay?"

"No!" I said.

"Hey, no judgments." And then he started laughing.

Richard and the professor approached the front door to the lecture hall together, both wearing blue jeans. "Maybe they're gay," I said.

"Maybe," he said. "As I was saying, that's the point."

"I have to go to class." As I went in, I glanced at the flyer, which invited me to a gay rights rally on the Diag that I'd never join. I stuffed it in my pocket, then took my seat, which had a good view of Richard's usual seat. Maybe now that we were friends, I could switch seats, sit closer to him, or next to him. My elbow might bump against his. It was too much to hope for.

After class, I thought about going up to Richard to ask what the Communist party line on blue jeans day was. But I lost him in the crush of students exiting class, and anyway, I had to get to my shift at the bake sale table on the Diag, for the *American Independent*. At least it could be a little factoid to tell my parents, a bit of proof that I was making friends, being social.

The managing editor from the mass meeting was there by herself when I arrived, with open boxes of cookies decorated with spider webs and cupcakes with orange frosting splayed out on a table in front of her. She didn't remember me, but she was friendly enough as she showed me where the cash box was, as well as a stack of fresh copies of the *Independent* to hand out to customers. I wondered if I was supposed to ask her for a date.

And then Jeff himself strolled up, looking dashing in a barn jacket with a brown corduroy collar. I wanted to say something to draw his attention, but I couldn't think of anything until I noticed he was wearing jeans instead of his usual khakis, so I asked, "Did you know about this blue jeans day thing or whatever?"

He chortled. That's the only word for the noise he made. Chortle. "Is it that time of year again? We ought to run a piece about blue jeans day. You interested in taking a stab at it?"

"Me? I'm not so experienced at writing."

"That's okay. Anyone can learn how to write. But it takes real cojones to think outside the box in this den of liberalism. You sure you don't want to try? Well, that's okay. You can contribute to our mission in other ways, like at bake sales." The way he said "bake sales" made it sound gayer than blue jeans. He popped a mini cupcake into his mouth. "Later, guys."

"Such a cutie," said the managing editor. "We ladies at the *Independent* drool over him."

I too thought he was such a cutie and wished I could also say so aloud. It seemed deeply unfair that I couldn't.

Fuck it, I thought. I am going to say it aloud. Though maybe not for her to hear.

At the end of my shift, I marched into the Student Union and asked for a copy of the local phone book.

❖

Lost Society was in a brick building with a fan-shaped glass window above the door, which was completely covered in posters advertising seasonal drinks specials and theme nights, as well as decorations for Halloween, grinning jack-o-lanterns and black silhouettes of devils and witches. I took in as much of it as I could while pretending to bend down to tie my shoe. Fumbling with my laces for a good while, I imagined what it might be like inside.

❖

The next day, I accidentally on purpose ran into Richard doing his flyering. Before I could ask his opinion of jeans day, he said, "Hey, I saw you raising money for the *Independent*."

"Yeah?" I blushed with pleasure because he'd recognized me. "They were having a bake sale or whatever. I was just helping out."

"You don't seem like you belong with that crowd."

"What crowd do I belong with?" I asked. "Haven't you noticed, I don't have a crowd?"

"You don't need to be in a crowd of any kind. You can be your own person."

"That gets lonely after a while," I said. "What about your group? Isn't that a crowd?"

"I don't think of them that way. We don't socialize. We work together on politics."

"Who do you socialize with, Richard?"

He shrugged. "Mostly my girlfriend."

I was stunned. Girlfriend? All this time, I thought he lived alone, that he was desperate for company. "That's nice," I said. My head was pounding, and my skin was flushing red all over. My stomach hurt as if I'd eaten too much frozen yogurt at the cafeteria. "What's her name?"

"Kimberly," he said.

Kimberly. It wasn't much to go on. What kind of girl could a Kimberly be? I wanted to size up the competition. "How long has... Kimberly been your girlfriend?"

"Why?" he asked, with the tiniest curl of a smile. "You jealous?"

Jesus, how could he tell? But then I quickly realized the question wasn't serious, just one of those things guys said. Guy talk. I was a guy, wasn't I? "Yeah, you wish," I said. It was a fairly convincing imitation of male banter, but it made me sad.

I was going to badger him with more questions, but Richard turned to offer a flyer to a kid walking by, and miracle of miracles, the kid stopped, and they began a long talk. This guy really was interested in Communism.

❖

The next afternoon in our discussion section, I was in a foul mood. Richard asked us about the Mexican-American War. It was one of his less terrible questions, about the War's underlying causes, which anyone could have answered if they'd done the reading. But as usual, no one spoke up. Richard rocked back and forth on his beat-up sneakers, leaning against the chalkboard, watching us, waiting, begging us with his beautiful glacial blue eyes to speak. Then he looked at me, silently pleading. Come on, be a pal. Be my pal. Say something.

Today, however, I didn't feel like being his pal. Why was the burden always on me to speak, to give the answers? Let someone else have a turn.

There we sat in a painful silence that lasted five, then ten minutes. It was like a dare. The other students looked at their hands, doodled in their notebooks, exchanged wry looks or giggled. Fifteen minutes passed, and no one felt much like giggling. A few of the kids turned around in their seats and urged me on with their eyes. I thought of Richard's girlfriend and looked away. Twenty minutes went by, then twenty-five.

I passed the time by brooding about Kimberly. What the hell could this "Kimberly" do for Richard that I couldn't? If they got married, how would they make a living? From Communism? News flash: Communism was dead, alright? And I was very much alive. Why hadn't he told me about Kimberly before? Maybe he was worried that if I knew, I wouldn't answer any more of his dumb questions in class.

Finally, mercifully, after thirty minutes elapsed, class was over and Richard announced that we could go. As we made our escape, Richard stood by the window and stared outside. He had such a hollow, pale look on his face, I feared he might cry. I wanted to get down on my knees, wrap my arms around his waist, tearfully beg his forgiveness, tell him how wonderful he was, how handsome, how idealistic, how true. He didn't deserve to teach a class of bratty kids like me. I wanted to pour out my whole heart to this man. Despite the fact that he never looked at me the way I looked at him and probably never would. Despite Kimberly. Despite everything. But I just allowed myself to be dragged out in the stream of students heading for the door.

❖

I carefully plotted my first trip to Lost Society, choosing a route with plenty of shadowy trees, alleys, and doorways where I could hide along the way. I'd chosen my outfit carefully—black T-shirt, black jeans—to blend into the night.

At the bar, there was a long line out front, right there on the brightly lit sidewalk where anyone could see. I circled the block a few times, and when the line got shorter, I ducked my chin into the collar of my fall jacket and stood behind a girl in a pink tutu and a guy in a white suit, a silver necklace with a peace symbol, coke-bottle glasses, and a long feathery wig.

After five unbearable minutes, I made it to the door, had my ID checked (18+ to enter, 21+ to drink), and paid my entrance. Inhaling deeply, I climbed up a flight of stairs and went in.

The bar was as dark as the *Independent* article had said, but maybe because this was a Friday night, the dance floor was crowded with guys, all wearing strange outfits, hats, and wigs, some of them in glittery masks. Was there a dress code? Then I saw a flyer taped above the bar. Tonight was a Halloween-themed dance party. How could I have been so clueless? I seemed to be the only one in the place not in costume.

I leaned against a pillar, midway between the dance floor and the bar, hugging my autumn jacket to my chest as I watched the men dancing or flirting with the bartender and each other. Unlike that mass meeting for the *American Independent*, when I'd been assaulted with friendliness, I was as alone as ever, still watching from the sidelines as usual, though in the dim lighting of the club, I couldn't see that well, especially from afar. You had to get up close to know what or who you were looking at, close enough to kiss.

Just do it, I told myself. Go talk to someone. Try to make a friend. But what could I say, what line could I manufacture to go up to some guy I'd never met and spark a conversation? What could I do or change about myself to get one of these men to look at me and speak?

The guy I'd seen in line, the one in the white suit and coke bottle glasses, was trying to squeeze past me with a drink in each hand. And suddenly I didn't need words. I stepped forward at just the right time, so he'd spill a drink on me.

"Oh, sorry!" he said.

"No, no, it's my fault. Let me buy you another one."

"You can't," he said, and for a second my heart fell. "It's just water."

We both laughed.

"I like your costume," I said. "Are you a hippie?"

"No, John Lennon," he said.

"Oh, of course, I get it now," I said.

"How about you? Who are you supposed to be?"

"Me?" I said. "I'm just myself."

"Cool, cool. Hey, you want to dance?" he asked.

So I joined him and his ballerina friend on the floor, where for kicks, they began singing out the lyrics to various Beatles songs and I joined in: "You Say You Want a Revolution," "Love Me Do," "Back in the U.S.S.R.," and "I Wanna Hold Your Hand." In between, John Lennon squeezed my hand, and then my butt. Though I wasn't drinking, I couldn't remember when I'd felt so high, so delirious, so fucking gay I wanted to flyer the whole campus with the news. I wanted to write an article about it for the *American Independent*. I wanted to call my parents to say that I was not a man for all seasons, just for this season, and from now on I was keeping my dirty nose quite definitely in the bars, thank you very much, especially if the bars were like this one. I wanted to wear blue jeans. I wanted to touch the thighs of conservative student reporters. I wanted to look up Communist Richard's address in graduate housing and serenade him with Beatles songs beneath his window until he finally wouldn't be able to stand it, and then he'd come down and beg me to stop, and I'd say no I won't, Richard, no, I won't ever stop singing until you take me in your arms and run your hands all over my body, and I run mine all over yours, and then you kiss me, passionately, deeply, full on the mouth as the seconds, minutes, hours run by, and we'd still be kissing and touching as if our lives depended upon it, until the seasons changed from fall to winter to spring, until we both ran out of breath, until the end of history itself, or at least the end of my history.

MARROW IS THE BONE

Laura Price Steele

Ben's faster on the downhill than I am. He stands up on his pedals, puts his arms out straight, and coasts without touching the brake. I can't do that—I'm always feathering the levers, even when it makes my tires shudder and skid.

The first time we ever rode together, he noticed me pulling up and he yelled at me over his shoulder. The words were muffled by the distance, by the wind, but I could tell from the way the syllables looped that he was telling me to keep up. I tried my best to stop riding the brake, but the momentum terrified me. It felt like my skeleton was going to slide right out of my skin. Even at my fastest, I couldn't keep up with him. I was maybe two hundred yards back when he fell.

I heard it—the tumble of the bike, the spokes rattling, and then the thump of a spilled body. The noise made my chest contract. Instinctively I closed my hand around the brakes. The bike tipped forward like a threat and so I opened my fist, let the wheels roll. Time elongated—I could feel the seconds stretch out like hot taffy.

When I came upon him, Ben was sitting up. The bike had careened off the trail and landed in the thick bushes down near the creek bed. I came to a skidding stop. Ben peered up at me. His helmet was cocked to the side and there was a smear of blood on his cheek. Of course we'd looked each other in the eye before, but this time was different. His embarrassment and my fear stripped the pretense off of everything, pretense I hadn't even realized was there.

"You okay, man?" I asked.

He smiled, looked at his gloved hands. "I think so," he said.

"What happened?" I asked. I expected him to take me through the play by play. That's the kind of guy he is—everything is a story to him.

Ben swung his gaze back up to meet mine and I felt a crumpling in my chest. "I fell," he said. His brow creased. He has one of those brows that's always creasing.

I swung my leg over my bike and set the back wheel against a tree. "You're bleeding," I said, looking at his cheek, but Ben glanced down at his shin. I took a step toward him and saw the thick red line on his leg. Without my bike in front of me, I didn't know where to put my hands.

Ben picked up a smooth rock, pushed it against his ankle and slid it up his leg so that the blood glommed onto it. Then he tossed the rock into the bushes. That made it worse, now the blood and dirt was matted into his leg hair.

"Do you want to try to stand up?" I asked. I held my hand out to him.

Ben smiled. He had the disheveled but satisfied look of a kid who'd somersaulted down a hill for no reason. He glanced at my hand and reached for it.

Ben and I had been working together for almost a year by then. We hung out sometimes outside of work—we'd grab a beer or go for a hike. We even planned to go skiing once, though we had to cancel when a windstorm kept the chairlifts from opening. But in all that time, all those hours unloading and scanning shipments at the warehouse, we'd never touched. That's what I realized when he reached out and grabbed my hand—it was the first time our bodies had ever come in contact.

I pulled Ben to his feet. We let our hands unclasp, but still he was only a couple inches from me. I could feel the heat coming off of him. It was the first time I understood him as someone with a body.

"Fuck," he said, looking down toward his bike.

"I can get it," I offered.

He shook his head and started down the slope. He had to wrestle with the bushes, which were so thick, his top half looked like it was floating. I could hear the sticks breaking against legs. He swore, hissing through his teeth. I sidestepped down a few paces and held my hand out and he rolled the bike into it.

Ben made a show of riding the rest of the way back to the trailhead, though the bike was making a rubbing noise like the tires were no longer set right. It was easy to keep up with him now, but I couldn't tell if he was riding more cautiously or if his bike just wouldn't fly like it used to.

He dropped me off in the parking lot of my apartment. I pulled my bike off the top of his car and he got the front wheel out of the trunk for me to reattach. I bent over for a second to set the fork on right and when I stood up, Ben clapped me on the back. It was not something he'd ever done before.

"Thanks, man," he said, leaving his hand on my shoulder. I thought for a second that he might lean in and hug me, but then his hand slid away.

"You better clean yourself up," I said. He still had a smear of blood on his cheek, but I couldn't tell where it had come from.

"The wife'll love that," he said, looking down at his leg. A beat of silence slipped by.

I smiled. "See you Monday," I said and I pulled my bike up on the curb.

❖

This morning Ben texted me one word. *Woods?* That's where we go most of the time. Wood's Gulch.

Okay, I write back. Our texts have been whittled down. It's like neither of us wants a written record between us. If I scroll up, it's just our history one word at a time.

Okay
Woods?
Here
Okay
8:30
Now?
Old Post
Where?
Sure
Blue Mountain tomorrow?
Got it
Left my hat
Here

Leaving
Running late
Here

Up in Wood's Gulch, the trees trap the night air, and as we ride up the trail it feels like we're hitting patches of refrigeration. I can almost keep up with Ben on the uphill. About a mile in, he looks over his shoulder at me and I can see that he is surprised at how close I am.

"Those long legs," he says. It's still strange to hear him name my body that way.

After that first bike ride, the texture of the air between Ben and me felt different. Walking into the same room as him was like stepping onto grass and feeling the subtle fist of a root—the reminder that hidden underfoot was a whole impossible network of veins that might stretch out for miles.

Nothing changed between us. We still talked the same, still let the conversation give way to the rhythm of the scanners as we unloaded shipments. For lunch we sometimes bought a pizza and split it down the middle. But all these things that had been happening all along seemed suddenly tied together. Ben noticed it too. We didn't talk about it at all, but I could feel the hesitation in his body, the extra breath before he spoke like he was considering how every word might fit into some larger context.

A couple months after that first bike ride, Ben invited me to a cabin for the Fourth of July. He and Katie had reserved a Forest Service cabin down in the Bitterroot. He told me at work as we sorted a shipment into soft bins to go out on the floor. Katie's sister and her husband were going. I'd never met them. But Becca and Nick were going too. I'd become friends with them through Ben, but I knew Becca from college too. We'd been in a few Lit classes together. They would be bringing their two-year-old son, Duke.

"If you don't have plans already," Ben said. He flicked open his box cutter and sliced the top of a box. The tape curled apart like skin.

"Only if I can bring my tent," I said.

"There's plenty of beds," he said.

I shook my head. I didn't like the idea of sleeping in a cabin where the only uncoupled people would be me and Duke.

"Okay fine," he said. "Sleep outside."

❖

I drove down the valley late in the afternoon on the Fourth. Already the cabin was strewn with sleeping bags and jackets and granola bar wrappers. The place had no electricity, just a wood stove and three sets of bunk beds. I understood that there would have only been enough room for me if some of the couples doubled up.

I was nervous at first that I would feel out of place with these people who were family or like family to one another. But as soon as I arrived I could tell that they had no interest in making me feel separate from them. They made room for me inside their closeness, though it was obvious that my place would be temporary.

We spent the daylight hours chopping wood, strolling down to the creek. I set up my tent in the grass on the east side of the cabin. Duke sprinted around the grounds and every once in a while he paused, looked toward the trees, and shouted "doggie." The first time it startled me. I held my breath and scanned for wolves.

"He thinks he can make them appear," Nick told me. "He shouts that when we see a dog, but it's like now he thinks it's the opposite—like the dog appears when he shouts."

Duke watched the trees for another moment, then took off toward the wooden fence. Still, I found my breath catching every time Duke shouted. Even after a half-dozen times, I couldn't help but look where he was looking, never quite shaking the fear that I might find a pair of eyes staring back at us from the shadows.

At dusk the mosquitoes came out. We slapped at our arms and legs, at the backs of our necks, smearing the tiny bodies across our skin. Ben lit the fire, hoping the smoke might drive them away. He was impatient about it. As soon as the flame came to life, he dropped a thick cut of log on top and snuffed it out.

"Shit," he said, picking up the log by one end as if he could undo the damage.

I stepped next to him, knelt down. I could feel his frantic energy. I picked up the sheaf of newspaper, crumpling up one page at a time and tucking each fist of paper into the center of the fire pit. Ben worked alongside me, following my lead. I put two big logs on either side of the paper and balanced small twigs across the top.

"Okay," I said.

Ben flicked the lighter. I wanted to tell him to light the paper from underneath, but it didn't matter really. It would all catch. The first burst of flame leapt up. Ben grinned at me. Of course that first flame meant nothing—it was only the paper lighting. The newspaper would turn to ash within a minute and we'd only have a fire if some of the wood caught too.

I picked up more sticks, ones no thicker than a finger, and I laid them into the sputtering flame. The wood began to crackle. Ben grabbed a splintered cut of wood from the pile. He reached it toward the fire, but before he laid it in, he turned and looked at me. He cocked his head and raised his eyebrows like he was asking for permission. Something pulled taut between us. I nodded and Ben's lip twitched into a smile as he set the log into the flame. We both stayed crouched there for another minute as the fire bit into wood and flicked up toward the sky.

All of us sat together for a while, letting the dry heat wash over our faces as the night closed around us. Conversation occasionally sputtered to life, but mostly we just stared into the fire. Duke fell asleep on Becca's lap, and she carried him into the cabin without saying goodnight. Over the next couple of hours that's how people disappeared. They stood up, looked up at the sky, down at the fire, and wandered into the cabin. Ben passed around a flask of whiskey.

By the time the night had settled into the dark dark, there were only three of us left—Ben and Nick and me. The heat from the fire and the whiskey made me feel like I'd been folded open. Even though my limbs were relaxed, I could feel an antsiness in my chest; I was waiting for Nick to go to bed. I did not know exactly what existed between Ben and me, but I knew that it could not breathe with someone else watching. When finally Nick stood up, I felt a rush up the back of my neck. Nick poked at the fire with a stick and the embers broke apart, their insides flickering bright orange. They looked alive. Nick dropped the stick into the fire and turned toward the cabin. I listened to him pull the door open, to his footsteps heavy on the wooden floor.

"Should we put more on?" Ben asked. The flames had nearly died out, but the heat coming off the broken embers would be plenty to get it going again.

I shrugged. I liked the way the darkness settled around us. Of course I'd been wishing for Nick to leave us alone, but now that he had I felt like I'd swallowed something wrong, like something jagged had lodged itself in my throat.

Ben pushed himself to his feet and settled another piece of wood into the fire pit. He leaned his face close, filled his lungs, then blew a long steady breath until a flame appeared. Ash dusted into the air.

Instead of going back to his spot, Ben came and sat next to me. He handed me the flask. I took another sip, even though my head was swimming. A long silence passed. I could feel my brain measuring the space between Ben's body and mine. Off in the distance a coyote yipped.

"Doggie?" Ben said, squinting into the darkness.

We both laughed. Ben curled toward me. He let his hand fall to the ground and the way it landed, his knuckles were just barely touching the side of my pants.

We stayed out there for another hour or two, let the fire burn all the way down. As the heat slipped away, the cold crept into me. When the embers had finally lost their glow, Ben stood up. He held his hand out and I let him pull me to my feet. I could feel the cords of his body pull tight against my weight.

"Do you want to sleep inside?" Ben whispered.

"I just have to find my tent," I said. In the darkness the space between things changed shape.

"Where's your headlamp?" Ben asked.

"I don't know," I said. "I think it's in the tent. Where's yours?"

"In the cabin," Ben said.

I looked up to the sky as if that might help, but all I saw was the sharp shadows of the trees and the dusty spread of stars.

Ben and I walked slowly, placing our steps carefully in the dark. The ground felt too soft, like it might swallow me whole. I put my hands out in front of me. It took longer than I thought it should to find the rough bark of the cabin wall with my palm. I traced my way to the door. Ben followed behind me.

"Night," I said without turning to face him.

"Your tent?" he said.

"I'll find it."

"I'm not going to leave you out here without a light," he said.

"It's really close." I kept my hand on the cabin as I walked. Ben stayed with me. When I reached the corner of the cabin, I tried to angle myself the right direction, then I took my hand away from the wall. It was darker behind the cabin somehow. My steps became more hesitant, my arms swam out in front of me. I thought Ben would stay at the cabin, keep his hand anchored so he could find his way back to the door, but instead he came with me. I could hear him breathing next to me, could feel the air move around him. Underfoot the bulbs of grass had the spongy but solid texture of a body.

We walked too far—I was sure of it. I swallowed, readied myself to admit my mistake aloud. But just as I opened my mouth, my foot caught on the edge of the rain fly, the nylon made a snapping sound and I pitched forward. My right palm pushed into the dome of the tent and I felt it start to give under my weight. That's when Ben grabbed me. One hand snatched a fist of my shirt and the other slipped into the crook of my elbow. He tugged me back, kept me from falling.

We both let out breathy laughs. Ben's hand slipped away from my elbow, but he still held onto my shirt.

"I found it," I said and he let out a breath through his nose like he was trying to keep from laughing.

I had to feel around to find the zipper. Ben let go of my clump of shirt, but he kept his hand on my body like he was still trying to stay anchored to something.

I crouched down and unzipped the rain fly. Then I reached under to find the tent door.

"Can I just sleep out here?" Ben asked. His fingertips rested on my shoulder.

"Okay," I said. I spoke without any sound, but Ben did not ask again. I unzipped the tent door and slithered inside. As I slid across the unfurled sleeping bag, the fabric made a whooshing noise like water pouring into my ear. I stilled my body as best I could because the noise threatened to drown out everything else. I waited, my neck curled, squinting at the open mouth of the tent door. For a second I thought Ben had changed his mind and turned back. But then I heard the thump of his shoes coming off, and he crawled in beside me. In the dark his body seemed much bigger than mine. He twisted, knocking into me roughly. Now that we were in the cramped cave of the tent, our limbs seemed to be fighting for space. Our clothes reeked of campfire. I scooted over to put some space between us. At the same moment, Ben and I both went still. The silence closed around us and we each waited for the swish of the fabric.

Neither of us moved. My body was tensed uncomfortably, but I did not want to shift, did not want to be the first one to make a noise.

"Goodnight," Ben said. The word came down like a boot.

"Night," I said and I felt a spidery sensation creep underneath my sternum. I turned on my side to face the tent wall. The edge of the sleeping pad hit me right on the hip bone. I tried to steady my breathing, but my lungs felt overinflated. Instead I took long, jagged breaths; the whiskey smell gathered like a cloud in the corner of the tent.

It was so dark that I had trouble telling if my eyes were open or closed. I blinked to test myself. Sleep seemed impossibly far off. The silence tunneled into my ears.

"You awake?" Ben asked. He said it so quietly I thought it possible he had not said anything at all.

"Yeah," I whispered into the wall. I moved my foot just slightly just in case he hadn't heard me.

I heard the slippery noise of the sleeping bag rubbing and then Ben's body leaned against mine. His forehead pressed into the back of my skull. I didn't know whether to turn toward him or not. His hand reached up under my shirt and he pressed it flat against my chest. It was almost unbearable, the heat of his palm, the solid heft of him.

As he burrowed his face into the back of my neck, I got nervous that there were maybe still bits of mosquitoes there. For a second I pictured them—those impossibly delicate bodies which I'd unceremoniously smeared into nothing.

I left before everyone else woke up. I thought the daylight might inject something awkward between Ben and me, but it was the opposite. We were too comfortable, and I knew it would be impossible to hide our intimacy from the group. It was like a piece of paper that had been folded—no matter what, it would never return to its original form.

Ben helped me take down the tent. I didn't bother to shove it back into the stuff sack. Instead, I balled it up and pushed it into my trunk. We didn't touch, but I could feel the imprint of where we had touched the way another person's gaze can bore into your skin.

When I drove away, Ben was standing over the cold fire pit, looking down into the dusty coals. If he raised his head to watch me go, he didn't do so until I was too far away to see.

❖

The first time I saw Ben after the Fourth of July was at work. Walking across the parking lot, I felt a churning under my sternum. I tried to let myself sink into the familiarity of the motions—swinging the door open, turning down the cement hallway and into the break room, clocking in. But I could feel everything had changed, like the world had become a mirror image of itself.

Ben was hunched over the warehouse computer. I pushed a box with my foot to make a noise.

He turned. "Hey," he said, but his eyes had that vacant look like he was addressing someone he'd just met.

"Hey." I picked up an empty box. Ben turned back to the computer.

For those first few hours it was like that—me just watching Ben's back, waiting for something. As I sorted the shipment into carts, I began to bury the memory of Ben's body. I could not forget it of course, but I could reshape it so that it was not he and I in the tent, but two strangers.

About halfway through my shift I had to go into the backstock area, where the shelves are pushed too close together and stacked high with bins. There is a handwritten note taped up that says *No Boxes on Floor*, but always someone has ignored it. It's easier to leave the half-full boxes than to try to find a place for them. I started pulling bins from the shelf to see if any could be consolidated. That's when Ben slipped behind me. I didn't hear him. When I turned he was there. He wasn't looking at me; he was staring at the shelf like he was trying to pretend that he was staring at the shelf. His shoulders were hunched up toward his ears.

I let my lips fall open. Ben didn't move. His stillness reminded me of a deer, of the profound silence that only an animal can possess. I waited, my hands on the edges of a bin. Ben didn't say anything, but his arm closest to me twisted in its socket just slightly, his hand opened like a bird spreading its wings.

I dropped my arm, let my hand fall into his. He wrapped his fingers around my knuckles and squeezed—one, two, three pulses. Though he didn't even turn to look at me before he slipped away, I could feel the clammy heat of his palm like a shadow on my skin for the rest of the shift.

❖

It's a steep climb up past the service road. Off to the left, the skeletal remains of the old ski lift come into view. Ben stops on the cut of trail that juts out from the trees. He drinks from the blue tube snaking out of his backpack. I can hear the whistle of the mouthpiece.

"How far do you want to go?" he asks, looking up at the sky. I follow his gaze to the v of a bird, which stays aloft without flapping its wings.

I shrug, spray water into my mouth. "Wherever."

We don't talk about the future, Ben and I. We never set any rules about what we could say or not say to one another. But after those first few times, when neither of us put words to what existed between us, it felt like we lost the chance. To bring it up now would require breaking through the layers of silence we've built.

We keep riding. The tree shadows become dark bars across the trail. I slip on a root and jam my shin down onto my pedal. My skin catches and even though I don't bleed, I have the raw sensation of being peeled open. Ben doesn't notice. I watch the yellow of his shirt disappear into the trees.

❖

Being with Ben lacks the perversity I've come to expect from sex. When we touch each other, it does not feel like a pantomime of what touching each other is supposed to be. It is like stepping off a stage I did not know I was on.

Those first few times, our bodies fell together like buildings collapsing. We did not speak, not at all. But still, we asked permission from each other. We touched one another so lightly, like we were handling rotten fruit, as if any firm grip might puncture the soft flesh we reached for.

I worried that the time between the sex would become stilted, but it was like something inside each of us unspooled. Conversation became looser, easier. When we were out at a bar or at work I added up all the moments I had to hold myself back, and alone together I counted through the list, pressing my hand along his jaw, rubbing my finger across the knob of his bare knee, burying my nose into his hair.

❖

Ben rolls to a stop at the top of an incline, puts one foot on the ground. He is breathing heavily, his arms slick with sweat. I make note that I want to cup his elbow with my hand. I will do this later, when we are protected by the dim light of my apartment.

"Should we call it?" he asks.

I nod. I never know how he decides it's time to turn back, but it's like a switch is flipped—he's done with the climb.

We turn our bikes around, dragging the back wheels across the trail. I fill my lungs like it is the last breath I'll get for a while. Sometimes the downhill feels like dropping underwater.

Within a few minutes of starting back, I can feel the distance stretching out between Ben and me as he curls over his bike and lets gravity pull him down the trail. The trees are singing by. The handlebars feel like they're disintegrating, like their atoms are coming apart at the seams. Instinctively, my hand reaches for the brake, but I don't close my fist. I let the tires roll, I try to find that marble in my gut—my center of gravity. Ben's yellow shirt comes back into view. His calves are long and lithe, almost too lean for his body. Maybe it's gravity pulling him down the mountain, but it feels like it's him that's pulling me.

When I see the gray blur come across my vision, I think the trail has somehow lifted up off the ground. That's my first thought—that the trail is rising up to meet the sky. But my eyes adjust and the blur comes into focus—I see the distinct outline of a body, one long furred muscle. Some wild thing in my chest comes alive. Before I can name the animal, I know it's here for blood.

A mountain lion. It's like some monster from a dream tearing into real life. I've never seen one in the wild, but I've seen the posters at trailheads reminding hikers what to do during an encounter—act big, make noise, never turn away, never run. I've come across the entrails they leave behind after a kill.

The cat has a bead on Ben. Its gaze is locked on him and the rest of its body moves around that tension the way water moves around a buoy. I know I can't shout; I can't do anything that would cause Ben to slow down. I touch the brakes just barely, to remind myself that I can.

For one long second that's how it is, Ben up ahead and the cat loping between us, taking great big uneven strides. The fear drops into me, but there is something else too, a sort of desire. It's like some part of me wants to see Ben hunted down and torn apart, as if the only way to truly measure something is to bear witness to its destruction.

The mountain lion gains ground, closing the space between itself and Ben. I worry that the universe is going to call my bluff. Panic surges through me. It's the sort of panic that pitches me out of my body so that for a moment I am myself but I am also the cat. I can feel its impossibly lean body, the spring-loaded heat of its joints, the soft knobs of its paws. For that brief second I can taste its hunger as if it's my own.

Without warning the cat slows for a step, letting its back legs catch up to its front, its whole body accordioning together. Then all at once it disappears into the brush. I don't know if it's given up or if it's finding a better angle of attack. Up ahead, Ben's sitting back off his saddle with his arms out straight. I don't call out to him. Stopping might be more dangerous than letting gravity have its way with us. I scan the edges of the trail waiting for that slender body to reemerge. I think about what it will be like to tell Ben this story later, how every part of him will feel different in my hands.

My gaze sweeps back and forth across the trail, waiting for the cat to come bursting through. The more time that goes by, the more I question the mountain lion's existence. I began to doubt whether I've seen anything at all. Then we are coasting down the last straightaway. Ben's body shudders as he hits the final log. He's good at letting his skeleton go soft. It's as if every bone in his body absorbs its fair share of the impact.

When we both come sliding to a stop next to the car, my fear morphs into a manic sort of pleasure. My heart feels like it has been blown apart into a thousand tiny versions of itself. I take a breath to keep myself from shouting the whole story all at once, but before I say anything, Ben speaks. "Finally stopped riding the brakes." There is something sharp in the way he says it, a little shadow of cruelty that passes between us. I nod, wipe the back of my hand across my chin. The sharpness passes. But already the wild thing in my chest is tucking itself away.

I don't say anything about the mountain lion. It feels too much like forfeiting something. If I share the story with Ben, it will no longer belong to me. It will be something he can take with him when he goes. The whole ride to my apartment I feel pressure behind my teeth as if my tongue has gotten too big for my mouth. I know that the second you start guarding against something, the more likely it is to come true, but still I can't make myself speak. Instead I keep circling back to that moment of recognition when the smear of gray turned into a beast—the white-hot terror of it. Over and over again I watch the body appear from nothing. At first I think my vantage affords me the best understanding of the scene; I can see the hunter and the hunted. But as we pull up in front of my place, I realize that I won't ever know whether the cat was really after blood or whether it saw something moving through the trees and decided to make a game of it.

CONTRIBUTOR BIOGRAPHIES

TJ BARNES's work has been awarded the Connecticut Book Award as well as a fellowship from MacDowell. Following a career as a studio musician and Tony-nominated Broadway producer in New York City, he now lives with his husband and their young daughter in Connecticut. In his spare time, he teaches writing to teenagers, supporting them in discovering their authentic voices, on and off the page. "Hospitality" is his first short story.

COLBY BYRNE is from Ridgewood, New Jersey, and graduated from Vassar College in 2018, where he majored in drama and minored in art history. During his time at Vassar, he wrote and collaborated on many original plays, and spent a semester studying theater in Moscow, Russia. He has since moved to New York City, where he's worked as a teaching assistant at a school for children with developmental disabilities. He spends his time writing short stories, and screenplays, in addition to studying Japanese in preparation to be a teaching assistant at a high school in Japan.

BILL GAYTHWAITE's short stories have appeared in *Subtropics*, *Chicago Quarterly Review*, *Grist*, *Lunch Ticket*, *Oyster River Pages*, *Atticus Review*, and other publications. His work can also be found in the first two volumes of *Hashtag Queer: An LGBTQ+ Creative Anthology* and in *Mudville Diaries*, a collection of baseball reminiscences published by Avon Books. He lives in New York City.

J.R. GREENWELL is a queer writer and playwright from Louisville, Kentucky. His works include two books, *Who the Hell is Rachel Wells?* and *In a Whirl of Delusion,* published by Chelsea Station Editions. He is honored to have been selected as a finalist six times and published in the Saints and Sinners Literary Festival anthologies. His newest story, "The Plump Cousins from Johnson City," is from his current work in progress, *The Boy Who Sewed (Tales of an Appalachian Sissy Boy).* J.R.'s memoir, *Teased Hair and the Quest for Tiaras,* an account of his early days as a female impersonator at the Sweet Gum Head in Atlanta, Georgia, and ultimately being crowned Miss Gay America 1979, is available online at www.jrgreenwellmga79.com.

AARON HAMBURGER is the author of the story collection *The View from Stalin's Head* (Rome Prize, the American Academy of Arts and Letters), and the novels *Faith for Beginners* (a Lambda Literary Award nominee), and *Nirvana Is Here* (winner of a Bronze Medal from the *Forewords* Indie Awards). His writing has appeared in *The New York Times, The Washington Post, Crazyhorse, Tin House, Subtropics, Poets & Writers, Boulevard*, and *O, the Oprah Magazine*. He has taught writing at Columbia University, George Washington University, and the Stonecoast MFA Program.

LISA HINES is a creative living and working in Philadelphia. She is passionate about story in all its forms, and has a singular goal with her work: to move the reader. When not endlessly filling 79¢ notebooks with attempts to do so, she designs interior spaces and is slowly restoring her classic Philadelphia row house. Lisa holds a Bachelor's degree in accounting from the University of Utah, and a Bachelor's degree in interior design from the Art Institute of Salt Lake City.

MORGAN HUFSTADER is a romance and thriller author and book marketer. She studied Creative Writing at Sarah Lawrence College and completed a writing intensive in Bath, England. She has since published seven paranormal and two queer contemporary romance novels. This native New Yorker is currently growing roots in New Orleans, where she lives with her lovely, patient wife and two eccentric dogs. She enjoys exploring dark themes and morally ambiguous characters and takes her iced coffee shaken, not stirred.

SAM NULMAN is a writer based on both coasts.

PATRICK EARL RYAN was born and raised in New Orleans, Louisiana. He is the author of *If We Were Electric*, a short story collection, winner of the 2019 Flannery O'Connor Award for Short Fiction, and published by University of Georgia Press. His work has been printed in *Ontario Review, Pleiades, Best New American Voices, Men on Men, Cairn*, and *James White Review*, among others. Previously, he was founder and editor-in-chief of *Lodestar Quarterly*. He lives in San Francisco.

CARRIE SMITH is the author of the Claire Codella mystery series from Crooked Lane Books: *Silent City*, *Forgotten City*, and *Unholy City*. She is also the author of a literary novel, *Forget Harry*. Her articles have appeared in *Writer's Digest, Daily Beast, Criminal Element*, and *Career Authors*. She has been a recipient of *Killer Nashville*'s Reader's Choice Award, a finalist in *Nimrod's* Katherine Anne Porter Prize for Fiction, and winner of three Hopwood Awards for Fiction from the University of Michigan. She is also a former fellow of the Fine Arts Work Center in Provincetown. Carrie lives on Manhattan's Upper West Side with her wife and adult twins. You can visit her at www.carriesmith.nyc.

WILLIAM CHRISTY SMITH holds a Bachelor of Arts degree in English from Westminster College, Fulton, Missouri, a Master of Liberal Arts degree from the University of Chicago, and a Master of Arts administration degree from the University of New Orleans. He works at the Jefferson Parish Library and lives in New Orleans.

ALISON R. SOLOMON grew up in England and lived in Israel and Mexico before settling in the USA. She is the author of four suspense novels which together make up the *Gulfport Mystery Series*. She has published short stories, articles, and chapters in numerous anthologies, textbooks, journals, and newspapers on a variety of topics related to feminism, LGBTQ issues, mental health, and Judaism. Alison has been active in multiple Jewish organizations and synagogues. In addition, she founded Gulfport Public Library's annual *ReadOut: A Festival of Lesbian Literature* in Florida. You can find her at www.AlisonRSolomon.com.

LAURA PRICE STEELE is a writer and editor. Though originally from Colorado, she now lives in Wilmington, North Carolina, where she earned her MFA from UNCW. She has been the winner of the Ploughshares Emerging Writer Contest in nonfiction as well as the Montana Prize in Fiction. Her work has been published or is forthcoming from *CutBank*, *Ploughshares*, the *Iowa Review*, and *Shenandoah*, among others. Currently she is working on a novel. You can find her at Laurapricesteele.com.

JOHN WHITTIER TREAT was born in New Haven and moved to Seattle in 1983, where he taught literature at the University of Washington for nearly twenty years before moving back to New Haven to teach at Yale. He has also lived in New York, San Francisco, Tokyo, and Seoul. His first novel *The Rise and Fall of the Yellow House* was a Lambda Literary finalist in 2016 and his short story, "Good Humor," was a 2019 Pushcart Prize nominee. Now back in Seattle for good, Treat is at work on a second novel set in the Pacific Northwest, *First Consonants*, the story of a stutterer who saves the world. www.johntreat.com

About The Editors

TRACY CUNNINGHAM retired after 25 years in education, having taught English, creative writing, and journalism, and began a career in event planning and nonprofit management. She is managing director of the Tennessee Williams & New Orleans Literary Festival, which hosts Saints and Sinners. She holds a B.A. in English Education, a Master's degree in English, and a Master's degree in Educational Leadership. She has been a national speaker and writing workshop leader for the National Writing Project, and is the Co-Director of the New Orleans Writing Marathon. Her writing has appeared in *Louisiana Literature* and in various anthologies and radio shows from the New Orleans Writing Marathon.

PAUL J. WILLIS has over 25 years of experience in nonprofit management. He earned a B.S. degree in Psychology and a M.S. degree in Communication. He started his administrative work in 1992 as the co-director of the Holos Foundation in Minneapolis. The Foundation operated an alternative high school program for at-risk youth. Willis has been the executive director of the Tennessee Williams & New Orleans Literary Festival since 2004. He is the founder of the Saints and Sinners Literary Festival (established in 2003). Willis received the Publishing Triangle Award for Leadership (2019). This nationally recognized award is for service to the LGBTQ literary community and was presented at The New School in New York City.

OUR FINALIST JUDGE

SALEM WEST serves as publisher of Bywater Books, Inc., a queer indie press out of Ann Arbor, MI. The company is comprised of its feminist and lesbian Bywater Books imprint, as well as the Amble Press imprint which focuses on publishing writers across the LGBT+ spectrum and queer writers of color. Previously, West was the voice of *The Rainbow Reader*, a highly successful review blog that combined original essays with insightful analysis of all genres of LGBT literature; and served on the Board of Trustees of Lambda Literary. She is active in the queer literary community and is a sought-after facilitator for groups, panels, and events focusing on feminist and queer literature. West and her wife, Bywater author Ann McMan, collaborated on the novel *Hoosier Daddy*, which was a Lambda Literary Award Finalist. She can be reached through bywaterbooks.com.

Our Cover Artist

TIMOTHY CUMMINGS, represented by Catharine Clark Gallery in San Francisco and Nancy Hoffman Gallery in New York, journeyed to a French Quarter pied-à-terre over-looking Armstrong Park in the Fall of 2017 as part of a My Good Judy Residency. The My Good Judy Foundation provides residencies for artists seeking to produce a body of work or performance in New Orleans that addresses culture making from an LGBTQ perspective. The residency was established to also honor the work of author and activist Judy Grahn. The subjects of Cummings' work are often children and adolescents struggling with issues of sexuality and sexual orientation in an adult world. In 2013, he was an artist-in-residence and subject of a solo exhibition at Transarte in Sao Paulo, Brazil. His paintings are also part of the collections of Whoopi Goldberg in Los Angeles, CA and Tomaso Bracco and Sara Davis in Milan, Italy.

Timothy enjoyed his time in New Orleans where he received inspiration from the spirits of his favorite writers Tennessee Williams and Truman Capote. "They shaped my early adolescence. They offer a magical telling of the spirit of this place. The darkness and humor of life and the queer Southern aesthetic shows up in my work as well. Williams' "garrulous grotesque, replacing the bleak mundane of the world with a lush queer poetic eye for the shadows is part of my focus," Cummings said. He graciously created an original painting of Tennessee Williams to be used as the cover art for the COVID-cancelled 2020 Tennessee Williams & New Orleans Literary Festival. We're proud to use this artwork for our 35th anniversary TW&NOLF virtual festival, and thank Timothy for the generous donation of this painting to the Festival's fundraising efforts. He resides in a tiny house in Albuquerque, New Mexico.

You can see more of Timothy's work at timothy-cummings.com.

SAINTS + SINNERS LITERARY FESTIVAL

The first Saints and Sinners Literary Festival took place in May of 2003. The event started as a new initiative designed as an innovative way to reach the community with information about HIV/AIDS. It was also formed to bring the LGBT community together to celebrate the literary arts. Literature has long nurtured hope and inspiration, and has provided an avenue of understanding. A steady stream of LGBT novels, short stories, poems, plays, and non-fiction works has served to awaken lesbians, gay men, bisexuals, and transgendered persons to the existence of others like them; to trace the outlines of a shared culture; and to bring the outside world into the emotional passages of LGBTQ life.

After the Stonewall Riots in New York City, gay literature finally came "out of the closet." In time, noted authors such as Dorothy Allison, Michael Cunningham, and Mark Doty (all past *Saints* participants) were receiving mainstream award recognition for their works. But there are still few opportunities for media attention of gay-themed books, and decreasing publishing options. This Festival helps to ensure that written work from the LGBT community will continue to have an outlet, and that people will have access to books that will help dispel stereotypes, alleviate isolation, and provide resources for personal wellness.

The event has since evolved into a program of the Tennessee Williams & New Orleans Literary Festival made possible by our premier sponsor the John Burton Harter Foundation. The Saints and Sinners LGBTQ Literary Festival works to achieve the following goals:

1. to create an environment for productive networking to ensure increased knowledge and dissemination of LGBTQ literature;
2. to provide an atmosphere for discussion, brainstorming, and the emergence of new ideas;
3. to recognize and honor writers, editors, and publishers who broke new ground and made it possible for LGBTQ books to reach an audience; and
4. to provide a forum for authors, editors, and publishers to talk about their work for the benefit of emerging writers, and for the enjoyment of readers of LGBTQ literature.

Saints and Sinners is an annual celebration that takes place in the heart of the French Quarter of New Orleans each spring. The Festival includes writing workshops, readings, panel discussions, literary walking tours, and a variety of special events. We also aim to inspire the written word through our short fiction contest, and our annual Saints and Sinners Emerging Writer Award sponsored by Rob Byrnes. Each year we induct individuals to our Saints and Sinners Hall of Fame. The Hall of Fame is intended to recognize people for their dedication to LGBTQ literature. Selected members have shown their passion for our literary community through various avenues including writing, promotion, publishing, editing, teaching, bookselling, and volunteerism.

Past years' inductees into the Saints and Sinners Literary Hall of Fame include: Dorothy Allison, Carol Anshaw, Ann Bannon, Lucy Jane Bledsoe, Maureen Brady, Jericho Brown, Rob Byrnes, Patrick Califia, Louis Flint Ceci, Bernard Cooper, Timothy Cummings, Jameson Currier, Brenda Currin, Mark Doty, Mark Drake, Jim Duggins, Elana Dykewomon, Amie M. Evans, Otis Fennell, Michael Thomas Ford, Katherine V. Forrest, Nancy Garden, Jewelle Gomez, Jim Grimsley, Tara Hardy, Ellen Hart, Greg Herren, Kenneth Holditch, Andrew Holleran, Candice Huber, Fay Jacobs, G. Winston James, Saeed Jones, Raphael Kadushin, Michele Karlsberg, Judith Katz, Moises Kaufman, Irena Klepfisz, Joan Larkin, Susan Larson, Lee Lynch, Jeff Mann, William J. Mann, Marianne K. Martin, Paula Martinac, Stephen McCauley, Val McDermid, Mark Merlis, Tim Miller, Rip & Marsha Naquin-Delain, Michael Nava, Achy Obejas, Felice Picano, Radclyffe, J.M. Redmann, David Rosen, Carol Rosenfeld, Steven Saylor, Carol Seajay, Martin Sherman, Kelly Smith, Jack Sullivan, Carsen Taite, Cecilia Tan, Noel

Twilbeck, Jr., Patricia Nell Warren, Jess Wells, Don Weise, Edmund White, and Paul J. Willis.

For more information about the Saints and Sinners Literary Festival including sponsorship opportunities and our Archangel Membership Program, visit: www.sasfest.org. Be sure to sign up for our e-newsletter for updates for future programs. We hope you will join other writers and bibliophiles for a weekend of literary revelry not to be missed!

"Saints & Sinners is hands down one of the best places to go to revive a writer's spirit. Imagine a gathering in which you can lean into conversations with some of the best writers and editors and agents in the country, all of them speaking frankly and passionately about the books, stories and people they love and hate and want most to record in some indelible way. Imagine a community that tells you truthfully what is happening with writing and publishing in the world you most want to reach. Imagine the flirting, the arguing, the teasing and praising and exchanging of not just vital information, but the whole spirit of queer arts and creating. Then imagine it all taking place on the sultry streets of New Orleans' French Quarter. That's Saints & Sinners—the best wellspring of inspiration and enthusiasm you are going to find. Go there."

—Dorothy Allison, National Book Award finalist
for *Bastard Out of Carolina*, and author
of the critically acclaimed novel *Cavedweller*.